Noël Coward

Noël Coward

Sheridan Morley

HAUS PUBLISHING • LONDON

First published in Great Britain in 2005 by
Haus Publishing Limited
26 Cadogan Court
London SW3 3BX

Copyright © Sheridan Morley, 2005

The moral right of the author has been asserted

A CIP catalogue record for this book
is available from the British Library

ISBN 1-904341-88-8 (paperback)

Designed and typeset in Garamond
Printed and bound by Graphicom in Vicenza, Italy

Front cover: photograph courtesy of Topham Picturepoint
Back cover: photograph courtesy of Marlene Dietrich Collection,
Film Museum Berlin

Contents

Prologue   1

The boy actor   3

For King and Country   13

Bright Young Thing   21

A frightfully depraved mind   30

A talent to amuse   39

Crest of the wave   47

Playboy of the West End World   58

A pretty exciting thing to be English   74

Surviving the peace   97

Future indefinite   103

Sailing away   124

Singing at twilight   132

Out in the midday sun: Jamaica   138

Epilogue   148

Chronology   156

Further Reading   172

List of Works   173

Picture Sources   175

Acknowledgements   176

Index   177

Prologue

Who needs another book on Noël Coward? There must be dozens, including no less than three of his own autobiographies and, I must admit, several titles of mine dedicated to his life, his plays, and even his paintings. But writing now, fully 30 years after his death, I believe there is something more to be said about him, and that 'something' derives from the work I have done in directing his plays and celebrating in cabaret and print his life with Gertrude Lawrence.

I seem to have been writing about Noël Coward for virtually all of my working life. Born within a few days of the last Christmas of the 19th century, hence the name Noël, Coward was a boy actor by the time he was 10. By 15, he had acted with the sisters Lillian and Dorothy Gish in D W Griffith's silent film *Hearts of the World*. At 20, he was a produced playwright, and by the time he was 30 he had written the drug play *The Vortex*, the epic 400-cast *Cavalcade*, the everlasting *Private Lives*, and the lyrical operetta *Bitter Sweet*, among countless other plays, revues and musical scores.

At 40 he had written, directed and starred in the Oscar-winning film *In Which We Serve*. At 50 he was painting, writing short stories and novels, singing in concert and cabaret, and starring in plays and films many of which he had also written and directed. By the time he was 60 he was famous as the jack of all theatrical trades and master of most, and when he died at 72, in 1973, it was already clear that he had represented not just the entire history of British popular theatre in his lifetime, but the spirit of the century.

He was also one of the kindest and funniest men I have ever known. When he first asked me to be the first to write his life story, he agreed that he would not even look at it until it was in print. I sent him the first copy of my *A Talent to Amuse* in 1969 and then waited in some trepidation for his verdict. It came as a telegram I still have framed above my desk. 'I am', it reads, 'simply wild about me'. Me too.

But in writing afresh here his life and career to make it fit within the strict framework of this remarkable series, I have therefore had not just to *précis* his life, but also all my own earlier writing about him, to fit a new format. I hope, therefore, that this will serve as both an introduction for non-Coward addicts and a brisk reminder for those of us who still believe he was the first and only Noël. I would like at this early point to acknowledge that this book could not have existed without the help of my friend and colleague Paul Webb, who brought a fresh vision and pair of eyes to me and to Coward at just the moment when I was in danger of being submerged by all my previous writing on the subject. This ready-reference guide will I hope tell you all you really need to know about the Playboy of the West End World, and his lyrics are quoted here by permission of the Noël Coward Estate and Methuen, who publish them in their entirety.

The boy actor

Nothing in Noël's life was quite what it seemed; the silk-dressing-gowned playboy pianist was in reality the son of a failed piano tuner from the wrong side of the Battersea tracks; the lifelong gay loner was all his life deeply in love (in every way but sexually) with Gertrude Lawrence; the passionate advocate of 'London Pride' and 'The Stately Homes of England' lived much of his life abroad, and the everlasting Peter Pan grew up all too swiftly.

Noël's talent was not only to amuse, although in writing his and my first biography I took the title from a song (*For I believe, that since my life began, the most I've had is just a talent to amuse*) but also a talent to disguise – at a very early age he had come to the conclusion that nobody really wanted to see him work, although work was always with him a kind of religion. When once I asked him the reason for this, he replied simply: *Work, dear boy, is so much more fun than fun.*

His mother's darling, the five-year-old Noël Coward

That work began at a precociously early age, as he recalled in his autobiographical poem, 'The Boy Actor':

I can remember, I can remember,
The months of November and December
Although climatically cold and damp
Meant more to me than Aladdin's lamp . . .
I see myself, having got a job,
Walking on wings along the Strand
Uncertain whether to laugh or sob
And clutching tightly my mother's hand . . .
I never cared who scored the goal,
Or which side won the silver cup,
I never learned to bat or bowl,
But I heard the curtain going up.

When Noël Coward died in 1973 he was as old as the century, and its most constant, if often controversial, show business figure. He left behind him over 50 plays, 25 films, hundreds of songs, a ballet, two autobiographies, a novel, several volumes of short stories and countless poems, sketches, recordings and paintings, not to mention the memories of three generations of playgoers on both sides of the Atlantic, for whom he had been the most ineffably elegant and ubiquitous of entertainers. Not altogether bad for a South London boy with almost no education, contacts or plans of any kind.

He was born on 16 December 1899, just before the last Christmas of the 19th century – hence the name Noël. The second son (his only sibling Eric) died as a young man of cancer in India, and seems to have been airbrushed out of the family history. Their father was an unsuccessful piano tuner and salesman, married to a doting, traditionally ambitious stage mother. Early in the 20th century, Noël grew up in genteel poverty at a series of addresses in suburban, lower middle-class South London – *I never had to gnaw kippers' heads in the street as Gertie Lawrence quite untruthfully claimed that she did, but nor was*

The boy actor in 1910, Noël had by this time made his stage debut and played a role in *Peter Pan*

my first memory the crunch of carriage wheels on the drive, because we never had a drive.

When Noël was 10, his mother answered an advertisement for 'a star cast of wonder children' to appear at the Crystal Palace in a play called *The Goldfish* – among the other children in the company were Miss Gertrude Lawrence and a Master Alfred Willmore, later more celebrated as the great Irish actor-manager Michael MacLiammoir. At the audition, Noël tap-danced in his own word *violently* while his mother played 'Nearer My God to Thee' on the piano, and a somewhat astounded producer, Lila Field, instantly gave him the job.

That led on to the role of Slightly in *Peter Pan* (Kenneth Tynan was to comment, years later, that Noël had been 'wholly in it ever afterwards') and Noël then settled, like his beloved new friend and soon to be dancing, acting and singing partner Gertrude Lawrence, into the life of a reasonably successful touring child actor. In his own view Noël was, *when washed and smarmed down a bit passably attractive, but one of the worst boy actors ever inflicted on the paying public.*

But these were the years of the First World War, when many better actors and indeed better-looking leading men were away at the Front, thereby removing much of the competition. Set against the constant economic and geographic upheavals of his home life, Noël's working career in these teenage times proved comparatively stable:

> *I cannot remember,*
> *I cannot remember*
> *The house where I was born*
> *But I know it was in Waldegrave Road*
> *Teddington Middlesex*
> *Not far from the border of Surrey*

An unpretentious abode
Which I believe
Economy forced us to leave
In rather a hurry . . .
I remember my cousin Doris in a party frock
With 'broderie anglaise' at the neck and sleeves
And being allowed to stir the Christmas pudding
On long ago enchanted Christmas eves.

Noël's teenage years were professionally and privately without any very secure centre. At home, his parents and brother Eric took to travelling all over South London from Balham to Battersea in unsuccessful search for lodgings they could afford, while as a teenage actor on the road, Noël himself was not so much tour de force as forced to tour.

He did however work with the best, and learnt his trade by slipping in to several rehearsals, even of scenes and entire plays that did not concern him. Just before the start of the First World War, Noël's longest run was as the pageboy in the last act of Charles Hawtrey's *The Great Name* at the Prince of Wales. Here, Noël realised, was the chance of an entire education in West End light comedy, and throughout the run Hawtrey was duly haunted by a small, adoring child who followed him around like a sheep, seizing every opportunity to chatter at him, get his autograph (17 times) or just stare at him. The effect on Hawtrey was convulsive. Not only did he once miss an entrance because the young Noël was talking to him, but he also began to believe that the child was really haunting him, and that wherever he turned in life, there Coward would be.

But however unsettling his effect on Hawtrey, the effect on Noël was precisely what he had intended – he learnt. He learnt about the theatre, about being an actor, and above all he learnt about comedy.

By the time Hawtrey's involuntary master-classes had ended, Noël was assured of his place among the small, select band of children (Master Robert Andrews, Master Harold French, Master Philip Tonge) who could earn up to £5 a week for their eager mothers by appearing on stage:

> *I remember the auditions, the nerve-wracking auditions:*
> *Darkened auditorium and empty dusty stage,*
> *Little girls in ballet dresses practising 'positions'*
> *Gentlemen with pince-nez asking you your age.*
> *Hopefulness and nervousness struggling within you*
> *Dreading that familiar phrase 'Thank you dear no more.'*
> *Straining every muscle, every tendon, every sinew*
> *To do your dance much better than you'd ever done before.*
> *Think of your performance. Never mind the others,*
> *Never mind the pianist, talent must prevail.*
> *Never mind the baleful eyes of other children's mothers*
> *Glaring from the corners and willing you to fail.*

By now Coward had established useful Christmas holiday and touring roles in both *Peter Pan* and *Where the Rainbow Ends*, and although the money, at around £5 a week, was still derisory, it was not a lot less than his father was making selling second-hand pianos.

In the summer of 1913, Coward appeared as the child desperate to be a pilot (*Please God bless Mummy and Daddy and make me a great big aviator one day*) in *War in the Air*, a theatrical spectacle. He had just come back to London from a brief trip to Liverpool and Manchester with Lila Field, appearing in *The Goldfish*:

Some of the children were strangers to me, but one in particular grabbed my attention. She wore a black satin coat and a black velvet military hat with a peak; her face was far from pretty but tremendously alive. She was very 'mondaine', carried a handbag with a powder puff, and frequently dabbed her generously turned-up nose. She confided to me that her name was Gertrude Lawrence, but that I was to call her Gert because everyone did, that she had been in The Miracle *at Olympia and* Fifinella *at the Gaiety, Manchester. She then gave me an orange, and told me a few mildly dirty stories. I loved her from then onwards.*

And so Noël had now met on that brief tour the actress and singer who was to be the other half of his working and private life for the next 30 years, and for whom he was to write many of his best songs as well as such plays as *Private Lives*, *Design for Living* and *Still Life* – which was later filmed as *Brief Encounter,* although of course with Celia Johnson and Trevor Howard rather than Noël and Gertie.

For all that, she was to remain his muse until her untimely death in 1952 and through so many of Noël's songs, not least

From the same childhood audition to individual stardom, Noël and Gertrude Lawrence remained as close as twins

'Someday I'll Find You' and 'I'll See You Again' it is possible to hear, albeit faintly, the echo of a love that could never be, for as we know Noël was lifelong gay and Gertie lifelong impossible. For all that, her importance to his life and work should not be, as it so often has been, underestimated. The last time he writes her (and she can been seen as both Amanda in *Private Lives* and Joanna in *Present Laughter*) is as the ghostly Elvira in *Blithe Spirit* and why is Elvira a ghost? Because his beloved Gertie had, early in the Second World War, gone to marry and settle in America, thereby effectively ending their quarter-century partnership.

Reasonably certain that 1913 was to be the last full summer before the war, Noël's entire family were taken by their aunts to the seaside at Lee on the Solent. There, as every summer, they would find Uncle George's Concert Party complete with The Poppy Pierrots who occasionally allowed Noël to join them on the sands for benefit nights: *I was born into a generation that still took light music seriously. The lyrics and melodies of Gilbert and Sullivan were hummed and strummed into my consciousness at an early age. My aunts and uncles, who were legion, sang them singly and in unison at the slightest provocation. By the time I was four years old, 'Take a Pair of Sparkling Eyes', 'Tit Willow', 'We're Very Wide Awake the Moon and I' and 'I Have a Song to Sing-O' had been fairly inculcated into my bloodstream. My mother and father were both musical in a light amateur sort of way but their gift was in no way remarkable. My father, although he improvised gently at the piano, never composed a set-piece of music in his life . . . I had no piano lessons as a child although my mother tried once or twice with singular lack of success to teach me the notes. To be born with a natural ear for music is a great and glorious gift. It is no occasion for pride and has nothing to do with concentration or will-power.*

Back in London after that first, hugely addictive summer season with the Pierrots, Noël now formed a curious, odd-couple alliance with Esme Wynne, a childhood friend; together they would raid sweet shops and, rather less criminally, correspond in a curious, secret language only ever understood by them. Prompted by Esme, Noël's desperate desire for attention now became one of the driving forces of his childhood. The first lines of his first autobiography show that this determination to be the central figure in the lives of relatives and friends had started very young:

I was photographed naked on a cushion very early in life, an insane toothless smile slitting my face, and pleats of fat overlapping me like an ill-fitting overcoat. Later, at the age of two, I was photographed again – this time in a lace dress, leaning against a garden roller and laughing hysterically.

As early as that, Noël must have stood out against the suburban tranquillity of Teddington like an exotic visitor from some already showbiz planet. Esme too was nothing if not theatrical, and it could be said – as she always claimed – that it was Esme who started Noël on his writing: *She egged me on to write*, admitted Noël, *and she was also the spur to my acting ambition, because I was madly jealous of her playing leads in* The Rainbow, *when I only had a small part . . . we even had baths together for the simple reason that we didn't wish to waste a moment's companionship and because it seemed affected to stop short in the middle of some vital discussion for such a paltry reason as conventional modesty.*

By now Noël was reaching an awkward age, too old to play the boy parts and yet too young for the juveniles. Nevertheless he stayed in work throughout the First World War, not least in his first film, a silent D W Griffith production shot on location in Europe and entitled *Hearts of the World*. Griffith, the great American pioneer of silent movies, had already made *The Birth of a Nation* and *Intolerance* and had come over to Europe to shoot a propaganda film about the German occupation of a French village which had both Lillian and Dorothy Gish in the cast. As it was designed to arouse anti-German feeling around the world (and *Birth of a Nation* had shown how suitable was the new silver screen for propaganda purposes), *Hearts of the World* was made with the full co-operation of the Allied governments. Griffith himself was taken on a lengthy tour of the French and Belgian battlefronts, at the end of which he remarked memorably that 'viewed as drama, the war is in some ways very disappointing.' When the cast and crew returned to England, Noël joined the cast:

I was paid, I think, a pound a day, for which I wheeled a barrow up and down a village street in Worcestershire with Lillian Gish. The name of the film was Hearts of the World *and it left little mark on me beyond a most unpleasant memory of getting up at five every morning and making my face bright yellow.*

Coward's colouring wasn't a weird whim of the director, but a reflection of the fact that lighting – and therefore make-up – on silent movies was far less sophisticated than was the case further into the 20th century, and as late as 1926, when Alfred Hitchcock had his first major hit with *The Lodger* (one of the few silent movies that is regularly screened on television today, and which was projected onto the outside of the National Theatre in July 2004), one of the main characters, a distinctly butch policeman, can be seen caked in make-up with eye-liner and lipstick.

For his part, Noël much enjoyed meeting the Gish sisters and their mother, but he felt he did not have enough to do in the picture, and also that the elaborate mechanics of silent filming had involved a disproportionate amount of his time for so brief an exposure on the screen. Another 17 years of his life were to elapse before he next appeared in front of the cameras, and then it was to be in the starring title role of *The Scoundrel* for Ben Hecht and Charles McArthur.

Back in the theatre, Noël toured in *The Saving Grace* and *Wild Heather* and then, while the family were moving Up West into Ebury Street, a small grey card arrived in the post – Noël was summoned instantly to an army medical at the Camberwell swimming baths.

For King and Country

My career in the British army was both brief and inglorious: you could indeed argue that a summons to the Camberwell swimming baths was not the most auspicious beginning to a career in the armed forces, and for Noël the nine months of 1918 that he spent on totally inactive service in and around Romford were one long disaster.

Even a cursory look at Noël's writing and performing during the Second World War indicates that he was not by any means unpatriotic or uncourageous. But at this time as an admittedly self-centred young actor, whose main priority was to get some money into the family and his mother out of the lodging house in Ebury Street as soon as he could, the war until 1918 had meant very little to him. When it started, he had been only 14, and now that at last it did affect him personally, the national feeling of optimism and determination had degenerated into an over-whelming sense of futility and waste that Noël felt more keenly than any of the hope that had preceded it. In this last winter of the war, it was hard to see that any good could come of the fighting, and the massive loss of life already seemed too high a price to pay for a still-distant peace. As he wrote later, *The needs of my King and Country seemed relatively unimportant compared with the vital necessity of forging ahead with my own life and career.*

Luckily enough, the King and Country took a similarly dim view of the usefulness of Noël to the war effort in these declining months of the conflict. From Camberwell he was moved on to a Labour Corps at Hounslow, and from there organised his removal to the Artists' Rifles, a well-known refuge for those of an unwarlike disposition. He still had to march around Gidea Park but, classified medically B2 because of incipient TB, was reassured to be told that he would never be sent abroad.

He did, however, manage to knock himself out by tripping on a loose slat while in mid-march, and awoke in the First London General Hospital to hear his mother explaining tearfully that he had been unconscious for three days and nights. Having convinced his doctors that this was no hoax, Noël stayed in bed for six weeks, surrounded by shell-shocked patients and nervously wondering whether he had given himself a brain tumour. Soon, however, he was well enough not only to start reading several novels but also to write one which, he said, *taught me two things. One, that it wasn't nearly good enough for publication and the other was that I had a certain knack for bright dialogue.*

When Noël was at length discharged from hospital, he eccentrically joined his old friend Esme Wynne and her future husband Lynden Tyson on a kind of pre-honeymoon, so organised by Esme as to avoid any danger of her getting pregnant. Noël then rejoined the Artists' Rifles, but was rapidly transferred, as his headaches began to recur, to the Colchester Hospital where he was placed inexplicably on a ward where all the other patients were epileptics. Alarmingly, none of them knew this, and Noël not unnaturally began to wonder whether he too was epileptic. For 24 hours, every 10 minutes he checked off squares in an exercise book; he did this twice a week for three weeks and only then, looking back over all the squares safely filled in, could he be sure of his own health.

If he was indeed inventing a series of slightly questionable ailments to avoid a war which even he, with his bleak lack of interest in current affairs, knew had to be in its closing months, he was hardly alone among the theatrical community. Eventually, after two months on the epileptic ward, Noël was given his total discharge from the British Army and awarded a pension of seven shillings and sixpence a week for six months. One suspects that he would happily have paid the army rather more than that for his freedom.

Once discharged, Noël went back to the lengthy round of auditions at which, dressed in a blue suit with matching shirt, tie and socks (it took him some months to learn that the height of fashion was not necessarily to wear everything in the same colour), he would give them a brisk rendering of his own early songs, including his first, 'Forbidden Fruit', and a sentimental ballad called 'Tamarisk Town'. Failing to find any work in London, he made several appearances with an amateur concert party entertaining wounded servicemen in Rutland.

By now, Noël always accompanied himself on the piano. It was another talent to amuse more or less self-taught; he had always found it difficult to read music and virtually impossible to write it down. When he played, it was by ear rather than eye and when he was composing he would either sing, whistle or hum the tune (often over the phone to someone like Elsie April who could transcribe it for him). Years later he reflected, *I have only ever had two music lessons in my life. They were the first of what was to have been a full course for which Fred Astaire and I enrolled in the early 1920s at the Guildhall School of Music, but they faltered and stopped when I was told by my instructor that I could not use consec-*

An early portrait of a precocious sophisticate

utive fifths . . . I argued back that Debussy and Ravel used consecutive fifths like mad. My instructor waved aside this triviality with his pudgy hand, and I left his presence for ever with the parting shot that what was good enough for Debussy and Ravel was good enough for me. This outburst of rugged individualism deprived me of much valuable knowledge, and I have never deeply regretted it for a moment . . . Acting and writing and singing and dancing seemed of more value to my immediate progress than counterpoint or harmony.

In that respect, Coward resembles Irving Berlin, born 11 years earlier. Both men were to become prolific composers of light music while themselves remaining only able to play it in limited keys. Both experienced throughout their lives considerable difficulty in either writing or reading even their own music. Perhaps for this very reason, both wrote songs that were melodically hugely simple and successful, precisely because their tunes were easy to pick up and repeat.

Noël was soon hoping to work for another great American composer, Jerome Kern, on a show originally called *Oh, Boy!* but which for the benefit of non-American audiences was retitled *Oh, Joy!* Unfortunately, in the pause before rehearsals began, Coward went to stay in Cornwall with a new friend, the novelist G B Stern, to whom he sent one of the telegrams for which he would soon become famous: *Arriving Padstow 5.30 Stop Tall and divinely handsome in grey.* Later, Stern was to dedicate her novel *Mosaic* 'to Noël Coward, with as much respect as affection, which is saying a very great deal'. But while staying with her his health, always precarious, gave out again and he contracted pneumonia.

The resulting week in bed on his return to London meant that he missed not only the first rehearsals but the chance for a character role. The management, annoyed at his absence, had relegated him to the chorus. Noël refused to accept the demotion and the management, who had after all already signed a contract offering him a decent part, now offered him instead a minor role in the play *Scandal.*

While waiting for this to start rehearsing, Noël began writing a novel called *Cherry Pan*, all about a daughter of Pan who, by the author's own admission, managed to be arch, elfin and altogether nauseating for nearly 30,000 words, at which point she petered out owing to a lack of enthusiasm on the author's part and a lack of stamina on hers. Noël's only published novel, *Pomp and Circumstance*, was not to be written for another 40 years.

Just before rehearsals started for *Scandal*, the Armistice Day of 1918 found Noël at the Savoy, listening to Delysia singing 'La Marseillaise' over and over again. The First World War had been for Noël little more than a gloomy background against which he grew through his teens: *When it began, I was too young to realise what it was all about, and now that it was over I could only perceive that life would probably be a great deal more enjoyable without it.*

By the late autumn of 1918, Noël's ambitions were, in no especial order, to be a composer, lyricist, novelist, actor and playwright, although all he had to show for that widespread optimism were a couple of unfinished novels, some songs and sketches in collaboration with Esme Wynne and one or two war songs which won him a valuable three-year contract to write lyrics for the music-publishing company then run in the Charing Cross Road by Max and Herman Darewski. For this, he got £50 the first year, £75 the second and £100 the third. But the firm displayed no interest whatsoever in any of Noël's own lyrics and quite soon after that went bankrupt. *A fact*, noted Noël ungratefully, *that had never altogether astonished me.*

His role in *Scandal* consisted of two brief scenes, in one of which Noël was costumed inexplicably as Sir Walter Raleigh. Perhaps because his role was not exactly crucial, Coward rapidly got bored of the play and its production and unusually his behaviour backstage left a good deal to be desired. One of the stars, Gladys Folliot, complained that he made rude noises behind her back whenever she appeared on stage, and he in turn counter-complained that her beloved dog smelt. Soon enough, Noël wrote a letter of resignation denouncing *the peculiar behaviour of certain old ladies in the cast* and hoping to resign in the nick of time before being sacked. The management however, were ahead of him and when he arrived at the stage door the next evening, he was given the rest of his salary and just half an hour to clear his dressing room.

For nine months Noël failed to get back into the theatre as an actor; but never one to waste time, even or especially when unemployed, he now wrote three new plays, all of which he sent to the impresario Gilbert Miller. Miller liked one of them (*The Last Trick*) and recognised in the still 19-year-old Noël, 'a man of many talents, over-sure of himself but a very hard worker'. Miller also taught Noël a few basic rules of playwriting, notably that the construction of a play is as important as the foundation of a house, whereas the dialogue, however good, can only be interior decoration.

Miller, acting then as an agent rather than a producer, managed to sell an option on *The Last Trick*, but failed to get any of Coward's early plays into production though one, *The Rat Trap*, did appear eight years later, albeit for only 12 performances at what was then the Everyman Theatre in Hampstead. But by the time Noël had finished them, he felt most importantly that *for the very first time I had the genuine conviction that I really could write plays*. By this time, though scarcely earning a fortune, Noël was helped out with the rent he was paying to his parents and other expenses by the regular cheques from the Derewskis and occasional sales of short stories, primarily to long-defunct women's magazines.

He was already a workaholic, and would spend most weekends as an unpaid pianist for hire at the stately-home house parties of his wealthier and more aristocratic friends. In these Stately Homes of England he found not only a future hit song, one that characterised his clenched form of musical satire, but a lifestyle of luxury far removed from Ebury Street, where he had moved to the larger room on the top floor. There, he would give tea parties for his friends, most of whom tended to mistake his father for the butler, understandably enough since it was he who served the tea.

Gertrude Lawrence now reappeared in his life with another ex-child-star of the time, Harold French, who later recalled for me Noël and Gertie dancing together impeccably at a new post-war nightclub in Old Bond Street: 'As early as this, we were all in slight awe of Noël – he had a very serious application to work which the rest of us somehow failed to share; he was always very friendly and yet somehow slightly removed from the crowd, as though he quietly knew he was going to do better than most.'

In the August of 1919, Noël finally returned to the theatre as an actor. Nigel Playfair offered him the leading role of Ralph in a production of *The Knight of the Burning Pestle*, with which he was opening the sixth autumn season at the Birmingham Rep. But the production was not a happy one, not least because Noël and a new friend, Betty Chester, managed to lose their scripts over the side of a punt. Noël by his own admission failed to understand the play in particular or Elizabethan comedy in general: *I mouthed and postured my way all through the play with little conviction and no sense of period* – a self-analytical verdict with which most of the critics seemed to agree.

His two weeks in Birmingham were, however, hugely enlivened by a cable from Gilbert Miller announcing that an American producer called Al Woods would pay $500 for an option on *The Last Trick*. Astounded, pleased and very much richer, Noël took Gertie to lunch at the Ivy and ordered a number of backless waistcoats of the kind currently made fashionable by the novelist Michael Arlen, one of a growing collection of writers, painters and actors whom Noël could now call his friends.

When 1919 was nearly over, Gilbert Miller returned from New York, sent for Noël and gave him the title and even the plot of a light comedy that he wanted written for Charles Hawtrey.

Within three days Noël had completed *I'll Leave It to You* and made sure of two things – that there would be a part in it for himself, and that Miller would guarantee a try-out at the Gaiety, Manchester. By now it was the January of 1920 and the beginning of the decade with which Coward was to be constantly and inevitably – if often turbulently and tumultuously – associated.

Bright Young Thing

The 1920s was the decade that made Noël, and with which he will always be associated in the public mind, even though it was at the beginning of the following decade, the 1930s, that *Private Lives* gave him theatrical immortality, and which also saw him triumph at Drury Lane with *Cavalcade*, the spectacular stage epic which demonstrated the patriotism that was to be so much a feature of his later work – on stage, on film and in songs – during the Second World War.

But at this time, he still had a name to make, and did so through a number of plays that established him without doubt as a Bright Young Thing of the period that went down in history as The Roaring Twenties. Noël was never one to roar, but he took advantage of a period of sexual and social freedom, and an explosion of youthful talent, that wasn't to be repeated or matched until the 1960s.

It wasn't to be an entirely easy ride, and the nervous exhaustion that conveniently saved him from the trenches during the war was to return, less opportunely, in the years ahead, as he later recalled: *Between 1920 and 1930 I achieved*

Noël at the end of the Roaring Twenties

a great deal of what I had set out to achieve, and a great deal that I had not. I had not, for instance, envisaged in those early days of the 1920s that before the decade was over, I would be laid low by a serious nervous breakdown, recover from it, and return to London to be booed off the stage and spat at on the streets. Nor did I imagine, faced by this unmannerly disaster, that only a few months would ensue before I would be back again, steadier and a great deal more triumphant than before.

The year 1920, which began with *I'll Leave It to You*, also saw his first trip abroad, while waiting for rehearsals to start. It was to Paris, accompanied by the first of the many male companions who were now to prove a constant feature of Noël's now discreetly but firmly gay life. They started off at the Ritz, though almost immediately (after they'd seen the first day's bill) moved to a more modest hotel for the rest of their stay.

I'll Leave It to You was a success in Manchester, where it opened on 3 May 1920, and it subsequently transferred to London, where it opened at the New Theatre (now the Albery) on 21 July, only there to prove a box-office flop, lasting just 37 performances. Despite this, Fleet Street reported that 'boy author makes good' and referred to him as 'an amazing youth', while at a press conference, when asked about his background, he snapped out *I am related to no one except myself* – a positively Napoleonic statement of his belief in his ability, if not destiny.

That his destiny was shaping up nicely was made clear in an interview with *The Globe – The success of it all is a bit dazzling. This may be an age of youth but it does not always happen that young people get their chance of success . . . I made up my mind I would have one of my plays produced in London by the time I was twenty-one, which will be in December . . .*

The rest of that summer was spent writing for two projects that were to go nowhere – a play called *Barriers Down* and the lyrics for an opera called *Crissa* – and was enlivened for his being arrested for 'vandalising' houses in Kensington (very Bright Young

Thing, and almost certainly after rather too gay a party) for which he was fined 40 shillings. The need to make money saw him back on stage in November, playing Ralph in Nigel Playfair's timely revival of *The Knight of the Burning Pestle* at the Kingsway Theatre, London.

The production closed by the end of the year, thanks to an attack of mumps that decimated the cast, including Noël, whose reviews had been tentative rather than enthusiastic – though *The Illustrated London News* thought that he 'wandered about delightfully'.

In the spring of 1921 he took a holiday in Rapallo, where he met the woman who was to design the majority of his stage successes from *The Vortex* onwards, and to become a lifelong friend and adviser, the also gay artist and from now on his closest theatrical confidante, Gladys Calthrop.

On 2 March of that year, he opened in *Polly With a Past* at the St James's Theatre, making the most of a small role against stiff competition from a cast that included Edith Evans, Edna Best, Claude Rains (later known for films like *Casablanca* and *Now Voyager* but at that date very much a stage actor) and C Aubrey Smith (also to have a starry Hollywood career).

Noël and Gladys Calthrop strike a pose

During the run of *Polly With a Past* he found time to write another play, *The Young Idea*, a satirical collection of poems which parodied the Sitwells, *A Withered Nosegay*, and to attend one of Ivor Novello's parties, where he met the American actress Jeanne Eagels, and decided he must try his luck in New York. Taking all his money and an aristocratic friend, Jeffrey Holmesdale (later Lord Amherst), he booked his passage on the *Aquitania* and set sail at the end of May, hoping to conquer Broadway with a bundle of manuscripts and just £17 in his wallet.

Jeffrey Holmesdale saw the sights of New York with Noël for a few days before travelling on (his peripatetic instincts made him Noël's most constant travelling companion well into the 1940s), leaving Noël to manage, alone, in a flat in Washington Square owned by Gabrielle Enthoven, a patron of the arts whose theatrical collection was to form the basis of the Theatre Museum in Covent Garden after her death. At this time she was able to offer the young playwright a free room from which to try his Broadway luck – a luck that seemed to have deserted him when all three managers to whom he had an introduction turned out to have left New York for the summer, in the days before air-conditioning when most of the city's theatres closed up for three months. It was, however, at this time he first met Lynn Fontanne and her soon-to-be-husband, Alfred Lunt, with both of whom he fell deeply if hopelessly in love and for and about whom he was to write *Design for Living* a decade later.

Depressed but undeterred by his failure to take New York by storm at the opening of his twenties, Noël spent the summer continuing to work on two new plays – *Sirocco* and the semi-autobiographical *Hay Fever*, based on his memories of hysterical weekend houseparties of compulsory games of charades at Laurette Taylor and Hartley Manners' home outside New York. Equally importantly, he made several well-placed friends, including Tallulah Bankhead and Ronald Colman, apart from Lynn Fontanne and Alfred Lunt. As Fontanne was to recall: 'Noël, who was then still precocious but somehow very brilliant, came to see Alfred and me with the script of *The Young Idea* . . . After that Noël dined with us every night because he couldn't afford to eat anywhere else, though we weren't so damned rich either.'

A vaguely sinister-looking Noël photographed on a cruise to Bermuda

But his immediate financial problems were resolved when a New York editor offered him $500 to turn *I'll Leave It to You* into a glossy magazine story – *For $500*, replied Noël, *I would gladly consider turning* War and Peace *into a music-hall sketch*. This income enabled him to move back into a hotel (he had been sleeping on friends' floors) and to enjoy numerous Broadway shows, returning to England at the end of October on a liner, one of whose other passengers was the sex therapist Marie Stopes. He had spent altogether five months in New York, was eager now to get home to London and more importantly bring to its stages and cabarets some of the vitality, energy and enjoyment that characterised Broadway. The pace of delivery of American actors was something that especially attracted him, and he was determined now to energise the London theatre with his own plays and performances.

But his return was to a period of unemployment, made manageable only by money from friends like Ned Lathom, a wealthy aristocrat and patron of the theatre – particularly if the theatre came in the form of attractive, young, gay men. Noël supplemented this with a couple of songs and an adaptation of a French play. Real money didn't arrive until the tour of *The Young Idea* began in Bristol in September, with Noël himself among the cast, despite the initial reservations of the producer, Robert Courtneidge.

While waiting for a London theatre to become available, Noël went for a Christmas holiday with Lathom to Davos in Switzerland, where Lathom realised that Noël had enough songs and sketches to make a revue. He duly summoned Andre Charlot, whose revue *A to Z* he had funded, to Davos to meet Noël, and the result, nearly a year later, was a show called *London Calling!* which included several of Noël's songs and sketches as well as the young performer himself making his revue debut in the West End.

The Young Idea opened at the Savoy in the New Year of 1923 to generally good reviews – 'the best comedy since *The Importance of Being Earnest*' said the *Sunday Chronicle* – but it ran for only

Noël and Gertrude Lawrence in *London Calling* at the Duke of York's
Theatre. 1922

seven weeks. His next project was *London Calling!* where he
was offered £15 a week by Andre Charlot (who didn't really
want him in the cast). He ended up with £40 a week, using his
part-author's right to veto major casting to blackmail Charlot into
meeting his financial demands, simply by refusing to accept
any of the proposed juvenile leads that Charlot offered. More
importantly in career terms, he also managed to veto contribu-
tions from many other writers, so that this already became a
Coward Revue in all but name. *London Calling!*, incidentally, was
the brand-new BBC Radio call-sign. It opened on 4 September
1923 – and with a matinée. The most successful of Noël's songs
was 'Parisian Pierrot' sung by Gertrude Lawrence, who was one of
the revue's stars:

Parisian Pierrot,
Society's hero,
The Lord of a day, the Rue de la Paix
Is under your sway,
The world may flatter
But what does that matter,
They'll never shatter
Your gloom profound,
Parisian Pierrot,
Your spirit's at zero,
Divinely forlorn,
With exquisite scorn
From sunset to dawn,
The limbo is calling,
Your star will be falling,
As soon as the clocks go round.

This was Noël's first hit song, and the first of the dozens he was to write over the next 15 years for his beloved Gertie. Its origins lay in Germany, as he later explained: *The idea for it came to me in a nightclub in Berlin in 1922. A frowsy blonde, wearing a sequin chest-protector and a divided skirt, appeared in the course of the cabaret, with a rag pierrot doll dressed in black velvet. She placed it on a cushion where it sprawled in pathetic abandon while she pranced round it emitting guttural noises. Her performance was unimpressive, but the doll fascinated me. The title 'Parisian Pierrot' slipped into my mind, and in the taxi on the way back to my hotel, the song began.*

The show received mixed reviews, the tenor of many of them being that Noël was a better writer than performer – something he reluctantly admitted to himself when the number he tried to put across, 'Sentiment' (with a dance staged by Fred Astaire), regularly brought the house down when performed, months later, in New York by Jack Buchanan.

Another sketch, 'The Swiss Family Whittlebot', was yet another send-up of the Sitwells, three upper-class siblings (Edith, Osbert and Sachaverell) who were famous for their avant-garde poetry and ideas.

After six months, Noël escaped eight shows a week in the long-running revue, which had already become something of a chore (he was always to hate, and decline, long runs), and returned to America. This was more of a holiday than an adventure, and it turned out to have been a necessary one, as he came back to a further period of unemployment, to a failed attempt to get Madge Titheradge and Gladys Cooper together to star in his play *Fallen Angels*, and to a distinct lack of interest among producers for another of his plays, *The Vortex*.

Undeterred, he wrote (in three days) a light comedy based on an eccentric thespian household's weekend – *Hay Fever*, the one that had been inspired by his occasional visits to the Laurette Taylor-Hartley Manners house in upstate New York. It was, however, rejected by Marie Tempest (a leading actress of the time, who was later to relent and star in it a year later), and Noël swiftly followed it with another of his earliest plays, *Easy Virtue,* seldom seen nowadays but intriguing in that it lays out, against the country-house background of which he had already become so fond, an essentially moral drama about upper-class British attitudes and their social consequences.

A frightfully depraved mind

The summer of 1924 saw Noël back on the country house circuit – staying at the grandest of addresses when he could only afford to do so by being invited to entertain other guests at the piano. That autumn afforded what was to be his biggest break: Norman Macdermott of the Everyman Theatre, Hampstead, asked to stage *The Vortex*. This was an ideal play for the mid-1920s: it caught the atmosphere of decadence, of hedonism, and of an upper class who seemed to have all the time and money they needed but nothing much of value to spend it on. To be fair, this was a metropolitan upper class whose values and lifestyle were almost unrecognisable

An early publicity portrait of Noël Coward

to the humbler majority of the population whose own virtues and values Coward was to celebrate in time of war – and when he was that much older. But theatregoing was at this time an elitist pastime, and there is no doubt that early audiences for *The Vortex* (which was to run on transfer to three London theatres for well over a year) took vicarious delight in recognising if not themselves, then certainly their weekending friends up there on stage. This was, if not a *roman-à-clef*, then certainly a piece of a *clef* in its tale of a beloved son taking to drugs in part at least because of his mother's infidelities.

For the moment, however, Noël was a young man with a name still to make and the best way of doing that (then as now) was to write a play that would be considered shocking. Sex sells seats, and *The Vortex* added drugs, toy boys and a hint of homosexuality, providing a stage that held up a mirror to the face of a section of society and revealing its – albeit fascinating – flaws.

This being the age of theatre censorship (which, astonishingly, wasn't to be swept away until 1968), Noël had to persuade the Lord Chamberlain that his was a play that deserved to be seen, and it was only when he was able to convince the establishment that *The Vortex* was, to all intents and purposes, a moral tract, that the necessary permission was finally given.

It originated when one night Noël found himself at a fashionable Mayfair nightclub with a young man who, across a crowded dance-floor, suddenly saw his own mother dancing suggestively with a man younger than himself. The play examines the life of a middle-aged society woman, Florence Lancaster, who has taken as her lover a much younger man, who is part of her son's extended social circle. The son, Nicky Lancaster, is a sensitive young man with a talent for playing the piano, who has been living in Paris, which offered homosexual as well as heterosexual pleasures. (Not for nothing was it known as Gay Paris. Among the royal family of the 1920s Prince George, Duke of Kent, was caught up in an affair with a young Frenchman, while love letters to him were bought by the royal family's agents in order to hush up the scandal.)

In today's eyes Nicky is clearly gay, and this subtext would have been readily apparent to the sophisticated metropolitan audiences of 1925, but Coward knew that this would never have got past the Lord Chamberlain, so he made his 'weakness' an addiction to cocaine. The drug was already wildly popular among

London's nightclub set, so its use in the last act of the play added to *The Vortex*'s contemporary feel. A classical edge was also achieved in the last-act bedroom scene between Nicky and his mother, a scene with a setting and an intensity that mirrored the closet scene in *Hamlet*. Noël was always an original but it remains the case that the two most famous scenes from his plays – the bedroom scene from *The Vortex* and the balcony scene in *Private Lives* – were both modelled on (or at least had very strong references to) Shakespeare's *Hamlet* and *Romeo and Juliet*.

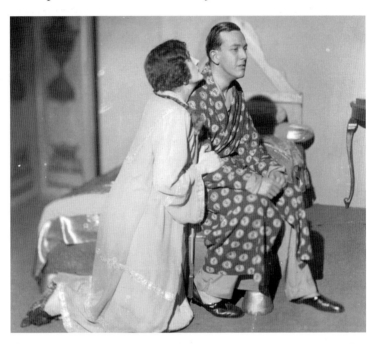

Noël and Lilian Braithwaite in *The Vortex*

Noël himself played Nicky, giving an intense, neurotic yet charming performance perfectly adapted to the character, and reflecting his own propensity to live on his nerves, a habit that would lead him to several nervous breakdowns in the course of his career.

The Vortex almost immediately became the talk of London, transferring first to the Royalty and eventually, in 1925, to New York, where it was to play at the Henry Miller Theatre and run for 157 performances.

Another Coward revue took place in 1925, *On With the Dance* at the Pavilion, while the same year also saw the opening of *Fallen Angels* and *Hay Fever* in London and *Easy Virtue* in New York. One of the songs featured in *On With the Dance* was a joky number about choirboys, and how the reality was very different from the angelic impression they gave old spinsters as they processed up the aisle on Sunday mornings:

> *We're six dirty little choir boys*
> *With really frightful minds,*
> *We scream and shout and rush about*
> *And pinch our friends' behinds.*
> *Nobody could admire boys*
> *With dirty hands and knees,*
> *But the countryside rejoices*
> *At our sweet soprano voices,*
> *So we do what we damn well please.*

Fallen Angels was written as a showcase for two female stars: Noël had originally hoped for Gladys Cooper and Madge Titheradge. Their parts – especially the scene in which both women get progressively more drunk – are better than the play, which some critics considered to be an over-extended sketch. The angels of the title, in the end, were played by Edna Best (then one of the brightest names in the West End but now largely forgotten) and Tallulah Bankhead, who took over late in rehearsals after Margaret Bannerman withdrew from her role following a nervous breakdown.

The play opened during a media storm about 'sex plays' and, though essentially light and jolly, it was exactly the wrong moment as far as the critics were concerned – two liberated women with a taste for sex and drink aroused a wave of indignation and reviews were dominated by words like 'degenerate', 'obscene' and 'nauseating'. Unsurprisingly this led to a stampede to the box office by a public eager to see what the fuss was about, especially if there was sex involved. There was a fracas in the stalls at the last performance, when a moral campaigner denounced *Fallen Angels* at the end of the second act, only to be drowned out by the theatre orchestra who, with a wonderful irony, struck up a popular tune of the time, 'I Want to be Happy'.

Noël joked about the reaction at the time, blithely admitting to *The Evening Standard* that *I may say I really have a frightfully depraved mind* . . . but when *Fallen Angels* was published he wrote a more considered piece on the role of sex on stage:

Rocks are infinitely more dangerous when they are submerged, and the sluggish waves of false sentiment and hypocrisy have been washing over reality far too long already in the art of this country. Sex being the most important factor of human nature is naturally, and always will be, the fundamental root of good drama, and the well-meaning but slightly muddled zealots who are trying to banish sex from the stage will find on calmer reflection that they are bumptiously attempting a volte-face *which could only successfully be achieved by the Almighty* . . .

Noël's next hit, *Hay Fever*, describes a weekend at the country house of an actress, Judith Bliss, her husband, son and daughter, in which four guests are subjected to an increasingly humiliating series of events, and discover they're just playthings for this talented but terrifyingly self-absorbed and mischievous family.

Having only eight characters and one set, it has often been assumed to be a relatively easy play to stage, but as Noël said, Hay Fever *is far and away one of the most difficult plays to perform that I have ever encountered.* Coward later claimed to prefer it to his later and better-known *Private Lives*, on the grounds that *It's quite extraordinarily well constructed. And as I did the whole thing in three days I didn't even rewrite. I enjoyed writing it and producing it, and I have frequently enjoyed watching it.*

Hay Fever opened in June 1925, as *The Vortex* (with John Gielgud now playing Nicky Lancaster) was in its London last weeks, and in his author's curtain call speech Noël noted that, whatever the critics would make of *Hay Fever*, it was undeniably 'clean'. Most critics in fact loved the play, though James Agate, as often, sounded a sour note in *The Sunday Times*: 'There is neither health nor cleanness about any of Mr Coward's characters, who are still the same vicious babies sprawling upon the floor of their unwholesome crèche . . .'

Easy Virtue had been written immediately after *Hay Fever*, in late 1924, and was the first of his plays to be premiered in New York. It was a light drawing room comedy in the tradition of Pinero and Maugham, a deliberate throw-back to an earlier age, and one which showed, to those who could look below the surface, that the *enfant terrible*, the representative of all that was young and modern in the theatre, was also, at heart, a nostalgist and, ultimately, a social conservative: *The narrow-mindedness, the moral righteousness and the over-rigid social codes have disappeared, but with them has gone much that was graceful, well-behaved and endearing. It was in a mood of nostalgic regret at the decline of such conventions that I wrote* Easy Virtue.

In 1926 Noël divided his time between writing and acting, with two plays opening in London – *The Rat Trap*, at the Everyman, Hampstead and *The Queen Was in the Parlour* at the St Martin's.

The Rat Trap had been written in late 1918, along with two other (unproduced) plays, *The Last Trick* and *The Impossible Wife*. It had to wait eight years before it was produced, in 1926, and even then it ran for only 12 performances at the Everyman. Coward described it, in print, as *my first attempt at serious playwriting. As such it is not without merit. There is some excruciatingly sophisticated dialogue in the first act of which, at the time, I was inordinately proud.*

From the point of view of construction it is not very good except for the two principal quarrel scenes . . . I think it will only be interesting as a play to ardent students of my work, of which I hope there are several.

The Queen Was in the Parlour was a Ruritanian melodrama originally written in 1922 when Noël was living in the country with his mother. It had two other titles before Noël settled on this one. His attempt at the Ruritanian style, made popular by Anthony Hope in his best-selling novel *The Prisoner of Zenda*, was not, as you might have expected, tongue in cheek, but in genuine tribute to a literary trend: *What was good enough for Anthony Hope was good enough for me . . . I was young and eager and . . . I thought, with an arrogant naiveté at which I can now smile tolerantly, that my brisk modern mind could fill old bottles with heady new wine.*

This Was a Man, written on holiday in Palermo in the late spring of 1926, and dedicated to the manager who was now his lover, Jack Wilson, was a comedy that Noël later described as *primarily satirical and on the whole rather dull*, but Basil Dean liked it enough to want it staged immediately after *Easy Virtue*.

The Lord Chamberlain thought otherwise, objecting to what he saw as disastrously loose morals – one scene in the last act, for example, features a moment when a husband, told that his wife has slept with his best friend, simply laughs. Today it seems dated and unthreatening, but in the late 1920s the Lord Chamberlain was adamant that it was dangerously modern, so it was produced exclusively abroad – in New York in 1926, in Berlin in 1927 and then in Paris in 1928.

In the course of the production Coward learnt a useful lesson, as he was to recall in a preface to a collection of his plays: *The fundamental error in the play is the second act which is a long-drawn-out dialogue between the wife and the ultimately seduced friend, both of whom are tiresome characters. If he had been written with less meticulous veracity and more wit it might have succeeded, but even so I doubt it. Bores on the stage, however ironically treated, bore the audience.*

As an actor, Noël toured America as Nicky in *The Vortex*, while in London he played Lewis Dodd in *The Constant Nymph* – giving his understudy, John Gielgud, a stressful time as he tended to turn up at the theatre with just minutes to spare, and Gielgud fully clothed and made up, ready to go on.

The Constant Nymph was an adaptation (by the director Basil Dean) of Margaret Kennedy's best-selling novel about the Sanger family. Noël was required, in the part of Lewis Dood, to completely change his appearance, with long hair, glasses, badly made suits and a pipe. This was

The stars of *The Vortex* take the boat train from Waterloo, en route to New York

a challenge for the director as well as for Noël, who informed a quizzical *Daily Express* that he'd taken the part *Because I wanted to see if I am any good as an actor in other people's plays.* As is turned out he was, despite a fraught rehearsal period in which he regularly threatened to quit, keeping John Gielgud on tenterhooks throughout.

Despite one or two continued worries and a playing time of three and a half hours, the play, Edna Best (the leading lady) and Noël all got good reviews, including this grudging acknowledgement of the range of his talents: 'You may like his plays or you may not, but this tribute you must pay him – there has been in our memory no stage personality who has achieved such success in so many branches of his art as this youth of twenty-six.'

Gratifying though this was, his nerves finally got the better of him after a fortnight and he spent an entire performance in uncontrollable floods of tears, after which a doctor was summoned, announced that the young man needed a complete break, and Noël set sail for New York, leaving a star-struck John Gielgud (*he knew how to hold the stage, and I felt he was a great star, even then*) to play the part for the next year.

Although *This Was A Man* was performed in Berlin and *Fallen Angels* went to Broadway, 1927 was to be basically a London year, with three plays opening in the West End – *The Marquise*, *Home Chat* and *Sirocco*.

The Marquise was a comedy set in the 18th century, written as a vehicle for Marie Tempest, who was duly gratified: 'Your writing of the play is, to me, amazing . . . I cannot tell you how much I love it all.' In terms of Noël's career this was a case of treading water, something he did a lot of on holiday in Honolulu before the play opened in London at the Criterion, to generally good reviews.

Noël was pleased by its success, while remaining fully aware that this was owed almost entirely to the performance of the leading lady, for whom this boulevard farce in fancy dress had been written: *To see her play it was for me an obviously enchanting evening, and has made me forever incapable of judging the play on its merits . . . If I could detach myself for a moment from Marie Tempest's personality and performance, I might perhaps see what a tenuous, frivolous little piece* The Marquise *is . . . read with disdain the whole play; sneer at its flippancy; laugh at its trivial love scenes and shudder at the impertinence of an author who, for no apparent reason . . . elects to place a brittle modern comedy in an eighteenth-century setting. But I am not and never shall be bereft of the memory of Marie Tempest {who made}* The Marquise *gay, brilliant, witty, charming and altogether delightful.*

A talent to amuse

Home Chat was written in the summer of 1927 and opened on 27 October. A comedy of supposed marital infidelity, it proved to be painfully slow – not least because Nina Boucicault, returning to the stage in the lead role after a long absence from the theatre, frequently lost her words, adding to the *longueurs* that were already making the audience restive. When Noël finally appeared on stage himself, he came up with a line whose immediate wit and sharpness, had it been more evident in the play, might have lead to a very different reception for *Home Chat*. In response to a yell from the gallery that 'We expected a better play!' Noël shot back, *And I expected better manners!*

The Observer agreed with the anonymous voice from the audience, wondering 'What is Mr Coward trying to do in this play? Is this farce or a comedy or a parody of what we call strong plays?'

Sirocco followed swiftly afterwards and was even more of a disaster, with a terrible first act that was so bad it went almost immediately into London theatrical folklore as a byword for overnight failure. It wasn't a good play to start with, but Noël had written it with Ivor Novello in mind, and given Ivor's box-office bankability, he thought that the play – essentially about the adventures of an Italian barman – would benefit from Novello's appearance in the leading role. And after all, hadn't Marie Tempest lifted *The Marquise*'s script and turned a very slight play into a gratifying success? Novello, who despite his reputation as an idealistic romantic was in fact a very shrewd judge of what would or wouldn't work on stage, turned the part down, and eventually only took it on as a rather desperate act of friendship when Noël threatened that he would play the role himself if Ivor refused. The idea of even the young Noël Coward playing a sultry young Italian barman was too ridiculous for words and Ivor felt that he had to save him from what would inevitably have been a public humiliation.

His sacrifice was more or less in vain, however, as *Sirocco* was a disaster from beginning to end. Ivor, meant to be playing a ladies' man, was even more than usually camp, and his love scene with the leading lady Frances Doble was so unconvincing that members of the public began making sucking noises as the actors embraced. Further commotion broke out at other key scenes, and at the curtain call the auditorium erupted in a storm of catcalls and boos. Unfortunately Basil Dean, the director, was a little deaf, and took the noise he vaguely heard for

applause, ordering the curtain to be raised again and again while the abuse from the audience intensified at this apparent act of ironic defiance.

Noël insisted on taking a curtain call as author – a characteristically brave thing to do – and this served only to inflame the situation. When he gallantly took Frances Doble's arm and offered her to the audience, a voice was heard to shout 'Hide behind a woman, would you?' Miss Doble, in the early stages of nervous hysteria, went onto autopilot and began her pre-

Ivor Novello and Frances Doble, in a publicity still from a more successful performance, *Downhill*. 1926

pared curtain-call speech: 'Ladies and Gentlemen, tonight is the happiest night of my life . . .'

This was a disaster so complete that it took on a certain glow of its own, and long after the play came off (which it very soon did), its title became a byword among the theatre community for a terrible flop.

Noël turned back to music in a major way in 1928, writing and directing *This Year of Grace*, in which he also appeared in New York. He wrote an unproduced screenplay, *Concerto*, and saw three of his plays turned into silent films. *Easy Virtue* was directed by Alfred Hitchcock, who had made his name with a silent thriller called *The Lodger* in 1926. This had starred Ivor Novello, who was also chosen to play the lead role in the movie of *The Vortex*, a film where, in order to soothe the sensibilities of the cinema-going public, apparently less accustomed to sophisticated depravity than theatregoers, Nicky's drug addiction was turned into a revulsion for anything to do with cocaine (his approach presaging Nancy Reagan's *Just Say No* campaign some 60 years later). Similarly, his mother's affair with a young stud, far from being a central theme of the play, was twisted and softened into being a mere infatuation, and one where she was worried that people might actually think they were (shock horror) lovers. The film was a travesty of the original play, and disappointed anyone who had read the newspaper reviews of the stage play.

Noël's next revue, *This Year of Grace!*, co-starred (along with Sonnie Hale and Laurie Devine) a huge-eyed young dancer called Jessie Matthews. She was to go on to be one of British stage and screen's most popular and highly paid performers in the 1930s before suffering an eclipse (partly due to a series of nervous breakdowns) that was not to be fully lifted until her late-life renaissance in the 1960s as Mrs Dale in the hugely popular radio series *Mrs Dale's Diary*.

Jessie, with Sonnie Hale, was the first to sing 'A Room With a View', which remains one of Noël's most popular songs – along with about a dozen others, from 'Mrs Worthington' through 'The Stately Homes of England' to 'London Pride':

> *A room with a view – and you,*
> *With no one to worry us,*
> *No one to hurry us – through*
> *This dream we've found,*
> *We'll gaze at the sky – and try*
> *To guess what it's all about,*
> *Then we will figure out – why*
> *The world is round.*

'A Room With a View' proved to be the hit song of the show, its popularity confirmed and given the royal seal approval by the Prince of Wales who, though he was occasionally bloody to Noël (reminding him that he was, fundamentally, an entertainer rather than a gentleman), nonetheless admired his music. The Prince had the orchestra play 'A Room With a View' nine times at that year's Ascot cabaret ball.

This royal seal of approval was a social success to match the critical one that *This Year of Grace!* received, with *The Observer* in particular giving it what Terence Rattigan described as 'the best notice ever written anywhere by anyone about anything'. Among *The Observer*'s observations were: '*This Year of Grace!* is the most amusing, the most brilliant, the cleverest, the daintiest, the most exquisite, the most graceful, the happiest, the most ironical, the jolliest, the most kaleidoscopic, the loveliest, the most magnificent, the neatest and nicest, the most opulent, the pithiest, the quickest, the richest, the most superb and tasteful, the most uberous, the most versatile, the wittiest . . .'

It may seem surprising that one of the other songs from the show should be a deeply melancholy one, but 'World Weary', which you can only really think of with Noël's voice in your head, expressed the other, darker side of him, the side that needed – as the lyrics suggest – regular doses of foreign sunshine to compensate for the grey English skies and the overwork that, ironically, paid for the luxury cruises that were its cure:

> *I'm world weary, world weary,*
> *Living in a great big town,*
> *I find it so dreary, so dreary,*
> *Everything looks grey or brown,*
> *I want an ocean blue,*
> *Great big trees,*
> *A bird's eye view*
> *Of the Pyrenees,*
> *I want to watch the moon rise up*
> *And see the great red sun go down,*
> *Watching clouds go by*
> *Though a Winter sky*
> *Fascinates me*
> *But if I do it in the street,*
> *Every cop I meet*
> *Simply hates me,*
> *Because I'm world weary, world weary,*
> *I could kiss the railroad tracks,*
> *I want to get right back to nature and relax.*

Noël's big hit of 1929 was the operetta *Bitter Sweet*, at Her Majesty's. This was Noël's very own *Tale From the Vienna Woods*, about a young heiress who elopes with her bandleader lover only to see him murdered by a jealous aristocrat. It featured some of his most attractive songs, including 'I'll See You Again' and 'If Love Were All'.

'I'll See You Again' has lyrics that perfectly match the elegiac tone of the piece, and was to be one of his most popular songs, frequently requested and still able to raise a tear when played or sung with a decent voice. There's no need to over-emphasise the emotion – in fact, underplaying it is the most effective way of letting music and words have their effect on latter-day listeners:

> *I'll see you again,*
> *I live each moment through again.*
> *Time may lie heavy between,*
> *But what has been*
> *Can leave me never;*
> *Your dear memory*
> *Throughout my life has guided me.*
> *Though my world has gone awry,*
> *Though the years my tears may dry*
> *I shall love you till I die,*
> *Goodbye!*

Similarly poignant and rather more personal was 'If Love Were All'. It gave Noël a signature song and me the title for a first biography (both his and mine), *A Talent to Amuse*. That he had, as his audiences were already well aware, but the sub-text, about the importance, impermanence and perhaps ultimate impossibility of romantic, sexual love, was one that applied to him throughout his life:

> *I believe in doing what I can,*
> *In crying when I must,*
> *In laughing when I choose.*
> *Heigho, if love were all*
> *I should be lonely,*
> *I believe the more you love a man,*
> *The more you give your trust,*
> *The more you're bound to lose.*
> *Although when shadows fall*

I think if only –
Somebody splendid really needed me,
Someone affectionate and dear,
Cares would be ended if I knew that he
Wanted to have me near.
But I believe that since my life began
The most I've had is just
A talent to amuse.
Heigho, if love were all!

On a lighter note, he also included a group of aesthetic young men, a reference to the willowy youths of uncertain sexuality whose symbol (before the Oscar Wilde trials blew the whole subculture out of the water) was a green carnation. In the song 'Green Carnation' they make their tastes plain:

Pretty boys, witty boys, you may sneer
At our disintegration,
Haughty boys, naughty boys, dear, dear, dear!
Swooning with affectation.
Our figures sleek and willowy,
Our lips incarnadine,
May worry the majority a bit.
But matrons rich and billowy
Invite us out to dine,
And revel in our phosphorescent wit,
Faded boys, jaded boys, come what may,
Art is our inspiration,
And as we are the reason for the 'Nineties' being gay,
We all wear a green carnation.

And that all of 60 years before 'gay' became a widely used and acceptable synonym for 'homosexual'. *Bitter Sweet* duly transferred to the Ziegfeld Theatre on Broadway, where Peggy Wood was replaced by Evelyn Laye, for whom Noël had originally written the score, and his work was also seen in the States when he contributed some sketches to *John Murray Anderson's Almanac*, at Erlanger's in New York.

As the 1920s closed, and with them his own twenties, Noël could look back on an astonishingly prolific and, overall, successful decade of work in which he had become not just a very popular actor and playwright, but a composer and a director, whose work was seen in the West End, in New York and other American cities, and on cinema screens throughout Britain. Not only this, but he had come to characterise an era, and the sort of bright, brittle, sophisticated, elegant and above all amusing man of the world that he was to represent, in public and usually in private, for the next 40 years.

And yet, as 1929 passed into 1930 and a new decade began, he had his finest moments ahead of him, and was about to star in the play with which he remains most closely associated – *Private Lives*.

Crest of the wave

Private Lives, with the second most famous balcony scene in all theatrical history (after *Romeo and Juliet*), was to be the epitome of Noël's wit and style. Just as the 1930s were more substantial and stylish than the 1920s, so *Private Lives* stood head and shoulders above his previous work. There was something less brittle, more grounded, more confident about the play.

Set in France, then still a useful shorthand for unconventional sexual behaviour, first on the Riviera and then in Paris, the story concerns a divorced couple, Elyot and Amanda Chase, who meet again, by chance, on adjoining balconies of a luxury hotel, where they are both about to begin their honeymoons with their new spouses, Sybil and Victor.

What is clear is that they're both still wildly attracted to each other, a fact that is explored as a subtext and then eventually comes out into the open. Harold Pinter, a great fan of Coward's writing, says that watching a production of *Private Lives* as a young man taught him that a playwright can have two characters saying one thing while clearly thinking about and meaning something else, and thus create two simultaneous conversations, one spoken, the other unspoken, but both heard by an audience.

Elyot and Amanda elope with each other that evening, abandoning their nice but dull newlyweds to their own devices. They catch up with them at Amanda's Paris flat, where she and Elyot are already finding it as impossible to live with each other as it is to live apart, and something in the electricity between them seems to spark off a similar row between Sybil and Victor.

The play included one of Noël's most memorable songs, 'Someday I'll Find You', sung each night in a rather cracked voice by Gertie Lawrence:

> *Some day I'll find you,*
> *Moonlight behind you,*
> *True to the dream I am dreaming*
> *As I draw near you I smile a little smile;*
> *For a little while*
> *We shall stand*
> *Hand in hand.*
> *I'll leave you never,*
> *Love you forever,*
> *All our past sorrow redeeming,*
> *Try to make it true,*
> *Say you love me too.*
> *Someday I'll find you again.*

There are recordings of Gertie singing 'Someday I'll Find You', and they make clear that though she may not have been the world's best singer, she had an undeniable theatrical magic. This captivated her leading man every bit as much as her adoring public, as he made clear in print: *Everything she had been in my mind when I originally conceived the idea . . . came to life on the stage: the witty, quick-silver delivery of lines; the romantic quality, tender and alluring; the swift, brittle rages; even the white Molyneux dress . . .*

Gertie has an astounding sense of the complete reality of the moment, and her moments, dictated by the extreme variability of her moods, change so swiftly that it is frequently difficult to discover what, apart from eating, sleeping and acting, is true of her at all . . . her talent is equally kaleidoscopic. She is the epitome of grace and charm and imperishable

Noël and Gertrude Lawrence, in her Molyneux dress, in *Private Lives*

glamour. I have seen many actresses play Amanda in Private Lives, *some brilliantly, some moderately and one or two abominably. But the part was written for Gertie and, as I conceived it and wrote it, I can say with authority that no actress in the world ever could or ever will come within a mile of her performance of it . . . Yet she can play a scene one night with perfect subtlety and restraint, and the next with such obviousness and over-emphasis that your senses reel. She has, in abundance, every theatrical essential but one: critical faculty. She can watch a great actor and be stirred to the depths, her emotional response is immediate and genuine. She can watch a bad actor and be stirred to the depths, the response is equally immediate and genuine. But for this tantalising lack of discrimination she could, I believe, be the greatest actress alive in the theatre today.*

Private Lives is a play that lives on the stage, not the page. *The Times Literary Supplement* described the text (published a week after the 1930 opening at the Phoenix) as 'so light as to be almost non existent'. But that, in essence, was the whole point. This play, probably Coward's greatest single claim to theatrical immortality, is as perfect a light comedy as Wilde's *The Importance of Being Earnest*, and as durable.

It is not meant to be read, but to be played, and as any number of stars (notably Elizabeth Taylor and Richard Burton, who on paper should have had a sure-fire hit with it but instead endured something of a Broadway fiasco in the 1980s) found, it is in the direction and playing that *Private Lives* stands or falls, not only on the fact that it offers two of the best star parts in all of 20th century British theatre.

Noël not only wrote and starred in *Private Lives*, he directed it as well. He took it to New York in 1931, the year *Hay Fever* was revived on Broadway and he contributed songs to *Cochran's 1931 Revue*. Among the songs for this were 'Half-Caste Woman' and 'Any Little Fish', but although the latter proved to be popular, *Cochran's 1931 Revue* didn't, and closed after some 27 performances.

The major event of 1931, however, was Noël's production of *Cavalcade*, which he wrote and directed at the Theatre Royal, Drury Lane.

Cavalcade was a complete contrast to *Private Lives.* Not only did it have a cast of hundreds and require the latest stage technology and the full stage and flying capacity of the Theatre Royal, Drury Lane, it was a historical epic rather than a small-cast domestic comedy. Inspired by finding a photograph of a troopship heading for the Boer War, seen in a bookshop on a page from an old copy of *The Illustrated London News*, *Cavalcade* followed the fortunes of one family and its servants through the first 30 years of the 20th century. In essence, the show had two driving spirits: to show that the British could write and stage big musicals at a time when Drury Lane was essentially under invasion from New York and Vienna, and to celebrate the essence of Englishness and the London pride which Coward already felt keenly.

Noël and his lifelong friend and designer Gladys Calthrop worked at his country house, Goldenhurst in Kent, from eight in the morning until five at night, with an hour for lunch, creating the script, sets and costumes. The production eventually opened at Drury Lane on 13 October 1931, a few days before the Labour government was replaced by a national coalition dominated by Conservatives. This was purely a coincidence, of course, but *Cavalcade* certainly revealed a patriotic and Conservative side to him that many of his worst

Noël photographed at his home Goldenhurst in Kent

critics would never have expected. During his author's curtain call on the first night he exclaimed, *It is still a pretty exciting thing to be English!* echoing the sentiments expressed on stage by Jane Marryot as she raised a climactic toast: 'Now then, let's couple the future of England with the past of England. The glories and victories and triumphs that are over, and the sorrows that are over, too. Let's drink to our sons who made part of the pattern and to our hearts that died with them. Let's drink to the spirit of gallantry and courage that made a strange Heaven out of unbelievable Hell, and let's drink to the hope that one day this country of ours, which we love so much, will find dignity and greatness and peace again.'

The first decades of the 20th century, recreated on stage in *Cavalcade*, had been momentous, and yet there was more trouble to come: but thus far Mussolini was no real threat, and the Nazis were not to come to power until January 1933. For all that, the new century was already fractured enough to justify Noël's world-weary 'Twentieth Century Blues':

> *Blues*
> *Twentieth Century Blues,*
> *Are getting me down.*
> *Who's*
> *Escaped those weary*
> *Twentieth Century Blues?*
> *Why,*
> *If there's a God in the sky,*
> *Why shouldn't he grin?*
> *High*
> *Above this dreary*
> *Twentieth Century din,*
> *In this strange illusion,*
> *Chaos and confusion,*

People seem to lose their way.
What is there to strive for,
Love or keep alive for? Say –
Hey hey, call it a day.
Blues,
Nothing to win or to lose.
It's getting me down.
Blues, I've got those Twentieth Century Blues.

Cavalcade has, ever since, been associated with uncomplicated patriotic fervour rather than world-weary sophistication, and that's entirely understandable, but Noël almost immediately came to regret his original curtain speech, as it helped stamp *Cavalcade* as, simply, a patriotic play rather than the epic piece of theatre, and extraordinary technical achievement, that it undoubtedly was: *This attitude I realised had been enhanced by my first-night speech – 'A pretty exciting thing to be English' – quite true, quite sincere; I felt it strongly, but I rather wished I hadn't said it, hadn't popped it on to the top of* Cavalcade *like a paper cap. I hadn't written the play as a dashing patriotic appeal at all. There was certainly love of England in it, a certain natural pride in some of our very typical characteristics, but primarily it was the story of thirty years in the life of a family.*

I saw where my acute sense of the moment had very nearly cheapened it. The Union Jack stretched across the back of the stage – theatrically effective jingoism . . . .With reasoning I felt better; better for myself, but sadder for poor Cavalcade, *It was already becoming distorted and would, in time, be more so. 'A message to the youth of the Nation'. 'A call to Arms'. 'A shrill blare on a trumpet', blowing my decent, simple characters into further chaos. I could stay in England and cash in if I wanted to, cash in on all the tin-pot glory, but I felt that it would be better for me, and much better for my future work, if I went away . . .*

And, as so often in the course of his life, he simply sailed away – with Jeffrey Holmesdale, his usual travelling companion, to South America.

In 1932 Noël reversed the failure of *Cochran's 1931 Revue* with one in which he was far more closely involved – *Words and Music*. This show, which played at the Adelphi, had not only sketches and songs by Noël, but was directed by him too.

It featured three enduring numbers, each of them reflecting different aspects of his public personality and private interests.

'Mad Dogs and Englishmen' was a satire on the British Empire – then still in full swing, having spread wider yet, after the costly victory of 1918, when the British absorbed Germany's South and East African colonies as well as getting more involved in the Middle East. The song poked fun at the upper middle classes who ran the Empire, but this was laughing at oneself from a position of strength – 'it seems a shame when the English claim the earth'. Ironically, once the Empire collapsed under the financial, political and social strains of a Second World War and the seismic shift that followed the Labour government's 1945 landslide victory, the song came to be seen as a celebration of a vanished world and a dying breed of Englishman.

> *Mad dogs and Englishmen*
> *Go out in the midday sun.*
> *The smallest Malay rabbit*
> *Deplores this stupid habit.*
> *In Hong Kong*
> *They strike a gong*
> *And fire off a noonday gun*
> *To reprimand each inmate*
> *Who's in late.*
> *In the mangrove swamps*

Where the python romps
There is peace from twelve till two.
Even caribous
Lie around and snooze,
For there's nothing else to do.
In Bengal
To move at all
Is seldom, if ever done,
But mad dogs and Englishmen
Go out in the midday sun.

More typically elegiac was 'The Party's Over Now' – a song referring to the end of a happy evening enjoyed by the 1930s version of Bright Young Things, but applicable to the end of any era, or of youth, or of a life . . .

The party's over now,
The dawn is drawing very nigh,
The candles gutter,
The starlight leaves the sky.
It's time for little boys and girls
To hurry home to bed
For there's a new day
Waiting just ahead.
Life is sweet
But time is fleet,
Beneath the magic of the moon,
Dancing time
May seem sublime
But it is ended all too soon,
The thrill has gone,
To linger on
Would spoil it anyhow,

> *Let's creep away from the day*
> *For the Party's over now.*

Another enduring song to emerge from *Words and Music* was 'Mad About the Boy', sung by a variety of women in a queue to see a handsome young matinee idol in his latest silent movie: Valentino and Novarro were likely candidates:

> *Mad about the boy,*
> *I know it's stupid to be mad about the boy,*
> *I'm so ashamed of it*
> *But must admit*
> *The sleepless nights I've had about the boy.*
> *On the Silver Screen*
> *He melts my foolish heart in every single scene.*
> *Although I'm quite aware*
> *That here and there*
> *Are traces of the cad about the boy,*
> *Lord knows I'm not a fool girl,*
> *I really shouldn't care,*
> *Lord knows I'm not a schoolgirl*
> *In the flurry of her first affair.*
> *Will it ever cloy?*
> *This odd diversity of misery and joy,*
> *I'm feeling quite insane*
> *And young again*
> *And all because I'm mad about the boy.*

There are several verses to the song, and Noël went on to write another especially for the New York production, though the management wouldn't let him put it in as it was considered too risqué, being sung by a well-dressed businessman rather than another adoring female:

Mad about the boy
I know it's silly
But I'm mad about the boy
And even Doctor Freud cannot explain
Those vexing dreams
I've had about the boy.
When I told my wife
She said
'I never heard such nonsense in my life!'
Her lack of sympathy
Embarrassed me
And made me frankly glad about the boy.
My doctor can't advise me
He'd help me if he could
Three times he's tried to psychoanalyse me
But it's just no good.
People I employ
Have the impertinence
To call me Myrna Loy
I rise above it
Frankly love it
'Cos I'm absolutely
MAD ABOUT THE BOY!

Playboy of the West End World

In 1933 there was a stage revival of *Hay Fever*, directed by Noël, as well as the opening of one of his most popular plays, *Design for Living* (which he wrote, directed and co-starred in opposite Alfred Lunt and Lynn Fontanne) and several films. These were the screen versions of *Cavalcade*, *The Queen Was in the Parlour* (retitled *Tonight is Ours*) and *Bitter Sweet*.

Design for Living has been described as the nearest that Noël ever came to writing a black comedy, differing from his other comic pieces in being less structured, but it is, like *Private Lives*, about people who can neither satisfactorily live together nor bear to be apart. What was so modern, and exciting, about *Design for Living* (and which necessitated it being launched on Broadway rather than in the West End) is that the play deals with a threesome, a love triangle between two boys, Leo (Noël) and Otto (Alfred Lunt), and a girl, Gilda (Lynn Fontanne).

Noël described the trio, who exist in their own artistic, Bohemian world, as *These glib, over-articulate and amoral creatures forcing their lives into fantastic shapes and problems because they cannot help themselves. Impelled chiefly by the impact of their personalities each upon the other, they are like moths in a pool of light, unable to tolerate the lonely outer darkness, and equally unable to share the light without colliding constantly and bruising one another's wings.*

This play went back to the very beginning of Noël's life. When, on his very first visit to New York in 1920, he had met another London exile, Lynn Fontanne, and her then lover (later long-time husband) Alfred Lunt, he had fallen mildly in love with

Noël, Alfred Lunt and Lynn Fontanne in *Design for Living*

them both and promised them a play. Now, fully a decade later they were understandably getting more and more impatient until finally on one of his frequent world travels Noël had received a somewhat irritable telegram reading simply 'Well, what about it?'

The result was *Design for Living*, recently and triumphantly revived by Sir Peter Hall, at the Theatre Royal, Bath, and in constant production around the world. It's a curious, untypical, amoral and often oddly touching drama which lies well outside the mainstream of Coward's comic writing, not only because it treats (albeit tactfully for its time) themes of bisexuality, but also because it is simultaneously more philosophic and less carefully structured than any of his other major comedies.

And yet, as always, there are similarities: like *Fallen Angels*, *Hay Fever* and *Private Lives*, it is about a group of people who find it impossible to live apart but equally impossible to live together, and like *Present Laughter* it is about the nature of the self-obsessed artist.

Noël knew that for his old friends the Lunts, and for himself, he would have to write a triangle. The play is about Gilda and Otto and Leo, who discover that, contrary to popular belief, three is not a crowd. Indeed they can only really survive as a trio: Gilda loves Otto and Leo, both of whom love her, but are also devoted, perhaps rather too devoted, to each other. You could even make the case that we are now very close to home: Noël loved Alfred who loved Lynn who loved Noël, and at the final curtain, all three come to realise that their unique design for living has, by its very nature, to be triangular.

As usual, Noël himself had the last word: Design for Living *has been liked and disliked, hated and admired, but never I think sufficiently loved by any but us, its first three leading actors. This perhaps was only to be expected, since its central theme, from the point of view of the average, must appear to be definitely anti-social. People were certainly interested and entertained and even occasionally moved by it, but it seemed to many of them 'unpleasant'.*

In 1934 Noël appeared opposite Yvonne Printemps in his own operetta *Conversation Piece*, in which he soon allowed her future husband Pierre Fresnay to replace him and in which she sang 'I'll Follow My Secret Heart':

> *I'll follow my secret heart*
> *My whole life through,*
> *I'll keep all my dreams apart*
> *Till one comes true.*
> *No matter what price is paid,*
> *What stars may fade*
> *Above,*
> *I'll follow my secret heart*
> *Till I find love.*

It could of course be realised that Noël's own 'secret heart' was in fact a gay one, but that was never a secret he was prepared to share with the press or his public at any time in his 72-year lifetime: Coward came of a generation and a world where private lives were just that.

In London that year he also directed *The Royal Family*, a waspish satire by Kaufman and Hart about a family of over-the-top theatricals not a million miles removed from the Barrymores, but one which had for obvious reasons to be retitled for the West End Theatre Royal. The following year, 1935, was a relatively quiet one for Noël, in which he wrote and directed his own Somerset Maughamesque drama *Point Valaine* at the Barrymore in New York without much success, and played Anthony Mallare in an American film, *The Scoundrel*, the first he had made since *Hearts of the World* back in 1917. This one was by Ben Hecht and Charles McArthur of *The Front Page*, a quirky and offbeat morality tale about a cynical publisher coming back from a watery grave. Noël felt that both he and the film should have been rather better, but it quickly became a cult success in the business. Adolph Green and Betty Comden would hold parties at which they acted it out scene by scene. Like so much of Noël's later work, it has also taken on a posthumous fame among the ever-increasing membership of the Noël Coward Society.

The year of George V's Silver Jubilee, 1935, was followed, in January 1936, by the old king's death. George V had been surprisingly popular ('I really believe they like me for myself' he told his equally respected but icy consort, Queen Mary) because he was a quiet, solid man who did his duty. His eldest son, Edward, Prince of Wales, was, by contrast, a highly glamorous figure who became both a friend and, at least until the Abdication, something of a role-model for Noël.

During the First World War the Prince had served on the Western Front, and though he was kept out of harm's way as best as the authorities could manage it, his driver was killed by a shell, and he saw the men's privations at sufficiently close quarters to be profoundly moved by it for the rest of his life. Books and articles have been written about his supposed traitorous tendencies, and it's certainly true that he had a soft spot for his German relations – 'German is my mother tongue' he proudly told various appalled

New York matrons in later life. Yet his desire to keep the peace with Germany, especially when it was threatened by the rise of Hitler in the 1930s, was something shared, at the time and without the benefit of hindsight, by many of his fellow veterans who hadn't hesitated to fight the Germans when called on to do so in the First War but were appalled at the prospect of a new generation having to go through the same hell in a second one.

In the 1920s Edward had been the golden boy of the British Empire. Pretty rather than handsome (he would have made an ideal lead singer for a modern boy band), he was highly photogenic, brilliant at playing a crowd and had an equally devastating charm in more intimate settings, though as Noël was to find out when he met him, this charm could be abruptly turned off and replaced with a very old-fashioned arrogance, completely at odds with his public image of an easy-going and informal modernity.

The glamorous youth of the 1920s (and Edward was to continue, until late middle age, to look far younger than his years) was to be replaced by an increasingly petulant and unpredictable Prince in the 1930s. Noël moved in circles that were very well aware of Mrs Simpson's hold on him, but to the public, the revelation of the King's infatuation came as a huge shock, and the King's self-imposed abdication and exile was the kind of shock unequalled to Britain's royalists until the death of Diana half a century or more later. In one sense it was the end of an England Noël had come to symbolise as the playboy of the West End world, but like so many others he knew he had to adapt to the new monarchical world of Edward's stammering, shy and less handsome younger brother Albert, who took the title King George VI. Fortunately it was his wife, later the Queen Mother, who had always been among Coward's most ardent fans and was to remain so until her death at over 100.

Noël, far from being shocked, was delighted at the turn of events. Unlike most of the country, he had failed to be impressed by King Edward from the start, and while many were mourning his departure, he suggested that a statue of Mrs Simpson should be erected on every village green as a thanksgiving for removing him from the country and the throne in favour of his duller but vastly more suitable younger brother.

While the death of George V and the abdication of Edward VIII dominated the public stage, the West End saw one of Noël's most ambitious projects to date: *Tonight at 8.30,* which he regarded as a way to revive something old – his stage partnership with Gertrude Lawrence

The Duke and Duchess of Windsor

– in the form of something new, a series of nine one-act plays, three to be performed each evening and six on matinee days. He wrote them in the course of the summer of 1935. This in effect meant creating a small repertory company with Noël and Gertie at its centre, and the considerable financial and artistic gamble paid off.

One of the few problems associated with the run – as usual, on tour out of town and then in the West End, in this case at the Phoenix, a theatre Noël had actually opened six years earlier with *Private Lives* – was Gertrude Lawrence herself. Declared bankrupt in the course of the run, she exhausted herself trying to raise money to deal with her remaining financial obligations, by filming *Rembrandt* with Charles Laughton during the day and acting in *Tonight at 8.30* each evening. Though some actors were able to keep up this sort of schedule from time to time (Ivor Novello in the 1920s, John Gielgud in the 1930s), the strain proved too much for Gertie and she had to take a month off, during which Noël, who was unable to carry on without her, temporarily closed the show.

Several new songs featured in *Tonight at 8.30*: *Red Peppers* was a tribute to and an affectionate parody of the sort of music hall/vaudeville acts that were already being decimated by the cinema and were, in the 1950s, to be finally killed off by television. A married couple, who professionally get billed a considerable way beneath the stars on the posters, do a drunken-sailor routine in 'Has Anybody Seen Our Ship?' The song has an authentic sound of the end of the pier about it and was yet one more example of Noël's ability to recall, in either satire or celebration, the musical theatre songs that he had first heard in childhood:

> *Has anybody seen our ship?*
> *The H.M.S. Suggestive.*
> *She sailed away*
> *Across the bay,*
> *And we haven't had a smell of her since New Year's Day.*
> *Heave ho, me hearties,*
> *We're getting rather restive.*
> *We pooled our money, spent the lot,*
> *The world forgetting by the world forgot,*
> *Now we haven't got a penny for the you-know-what!*
> *Has anybody seen our ship?*

The other song in *Red Peppers* is the top-hat-and-tails 'Men About Town' which would have been a perfect fit at this time for Fred Astaire and Ginger Rogers, while in *Shadow Play*, another of these seldom-revived one-acters, there was the haunting 'You Were There' which, although still curiously unknown, seems to me perfectly to capture that sense, as in all Noël's best non-comic numbers, of a love which somehow (whether sexually or simply geographically) can never be reached or even recaptured:

You were there,
I saw you and my heart stopped beating,
You were there
And in that first enchanted meeting
Life changed its tune,
The stars, the moon
Came near to me.
Dreams that I dreamed,
Like magic seemed
To be clear to me, dear to me.
You were there.
Your eyes looked into mine and faltered.
Everywhere
The colour of the whole world altered.
False became true,
My universe tumbled in two,
The earth became heaven, for you
Were there.

As Noël himself once said to me, *Don't tell me that just because I am gay I have never loved women: nobody who truly loves the theatre can fail to love women. I just don't love them in what is known as 'that way'.*

But although *Tonight at 8.30* was unparalleled in its sheer ambition (a resident company of less than a dozen rotating these nine plays and mini-musicals, one of the former becoming a decade later the classic movie *Brief Encounter*), the initial 1936 reviews were not exactly wild with enthusiasm. *The Times* considered that *The Astonished Heart* 'didn't quite work, despite it being genuinely imaginative', but it enjoyed *Red Peppers*, where it thought 'Mr Coward the dramatist is comfortably within his range' and thought that, as an actor, he 'knows how, together with Miss Lawrence, to make the most of his own swift nonsense. It was a robust end to an otherwise slim . . . entertainment.' Interestingly the review also singled out Noël's dancing ability – one of the few stage accomplishments for which he is not particularly well remembered nowadays.

The Daily Mail also thought *Red Peppers* was the most successful play, if only for the rather (in its opinion) slapstick nature of its appeal: 'Mr Noël Coward . . . wore a sailor suit and a red nose . . . Naturally, in the same way as Mr Shaw would be a success if he cared to appear on the halls as a tramp-cyclist, this brought the evening to a happy conclusion.'

In the first quarter of the 20th century, with a few distinguished exceptions among the works of Bernard Shaw and J M Barrie, the one-act play had fallen on hard times. In the regions, some were still being done as under-cast, ill-produced curtain-raisers, but in the West End, the form had disappeared altogether as the result of a widespread managerial belief that the public did not come to see double or triple bills, because they felt paradoxically they would be getting less value for money.

Noël, as so often, took a contrary view: *The one-act play has a great advantage over a long one, in that it can sustain a mood without technical creaking or over-padding. It deserves a better fate, and if by careful writing, acting and producing I can do a little toward re-instating it in its rightful pride I shall have achieved one of my more sentimental ambitions.*

These nine plays were also intriguing for the way in which they reflected Noël's multiple and often apparently contradictory personalities as both writer and actor, dancer and singer. Some, like *Shadow Play* and *We Were Dancing*, were deliberate throwbacks to the elegant, wistful mood of *Private Lives*. But then again there was backstage farce (*Red Peppers*), suburban marital distress (*Fumed Oak*) and of course the most famous of them all, *Still Life*.

Most of these plays served as a useful reminder that Coward was capable of writing not only about the rich and glamorous predecessors of the Beautiful People, among whom the vast majority of his early plays were set. And looking ahead, *Shadow*

Play uses a series of highly cinematic techniques, such as flash-backs and disconnected scenes played quickly in pools of light to make up the theatrical equivalent of a montage.

But perhaps the most astonishing of all these nine plays was *The Astonished Heart*, a one-act melodrama which Noël was, after the war, to film, not entirely successfully, despite a cast including Margaret Leighton and Celia Johnson.

Noël himself on stage and screen played the central figure, a psychiatrist driven mad and then to his death by his inability to choose between a wife and a mistress. Hackneyed as that theme may now sound, it genuinely shocked audiences who were accustomed to seeing Noël elegantly trading quips with Gertie through clenched cigarette holders on hotel balconies. Here he was, still with Gertie but this time in a play about a man literally dying for love – and a psychiatrist at that.

The following year, 1937, saw the coronation of King George VI and on the Coward front, the publication of his first and best book of memoirs, *Present Indicative.* As so often with the autobiographies of theatre folk (Moss Hart and Emelyn Williams, to name but two), the best chapters are always the ones that deal with childhood and here Noël's own recollection of his proud, lower middle-class suburban relatives was intensely evocative of an already vanished world.

This is the only place in which Noël lays out the pattern of his life and explains the rules by which it was to be lived. The Teddington boyhood of genteel poverty, the failed father, the ambitious mother taking in lodgers to keep the family afloat, the child-actor meeting with Gertrude Lawrence, the desperate determination to succeed so that success could be a passport out of a suburban world he did not care for, the survival of failure and loneliness, the early passion for travel, preferably by sea, the belief in work as a kind of religious discipline, the delighted discovery of the urgent pace and intensity of New York, and then at 24 the success with *The Vortex* that was to change his life and the face of London for him: all that is what *Present Indicative* is all about.

Noël himself was, as so often, one of the book's sharpest critics: *The style is sometimes convulsive, there are too many qualifying adjectives, it is technically insecure and there are several repetitive passages which slow up the narrative; but on the whole there is little in it that I regret having said. From it there emerges enough of my true character to make it valid . . . for as long as it is in print, or obtainable from second-hand bookshops, there will be people (probably in diminishing numbers) who will be fascinated or repelled, charmed or unimpressed by the story of an alert little boy who was talented and determined and grew up to attain a surprising number of his heart's desires.*

But *Present Indicative* has always attracted Noël's critics as well as his admirers. Cyril Connolly, for instance, writing in the *New Statesman*, of the original edition: 'It is almost always shallow, and often dull, and leaves us with the picture, carefully incomplete, of one of the most talented and prodigiously successful people the world has ever known. A person of infinite charm and adaptability whose very adaptability however makes him inferior to a more compact and worldly competitor in his own sphere, like Cole Porter. This is an essentially unhappy man who gives the impression of having seldom really thought or really lived, and who is intelligent enough to know it. But what is Coward to do? He is not religious, politics bore him, art means facility or else brickbats, love is only wild excitement or the nervous breakdown. There is only success, more and more of it, 'til from his pinnacle he can look down on Ivor Novello, Beverly Nichols and Godfrey Winn. But success is all there is and even that is temporary, for one can't read any of Coward's plays now . . . they are written in the most topical and perishable way imaginable and the cream in them turns sour overnight. They are even dead before they are turned into talkies, however engaging they may seem at the time. This autobiography reveals a terrible predicament, that of a young man with the Midas touch, a gift that does not creep or branch or flower, but which turns everything into immediate gold. But the gold melts.'

Luckily for Noël, there was always another country where his gifts were less critically considered and the offers of work remained undiminished. In America he directed Gerald Savory's *George and Margaret* at the Morosco on Broadway.

In 1938 Noël had another excursion into musical theatre, with *Operette,* which he wrote and directed, and which opened at His Majesty's in London. The show included the satirical number 'The Stately Homes of England' and the deeply nostalgic 'Where Are the Songs We Sung', demonstrating yet again his versatility as a composer of comic and poignant popular songs, and his ability to capture the mood of the moment. His hope had always been to repeat the operetta success he had had with *Bitter Sweet,* but here as with *Conversation Piece* the hope was to remain just that.

The cover of the 'Stately Homes' score sheet

Why? *Operette* was perhaps overwritten and underco posed, producing a complex book that the songs were not able to support; the plot even included a play-within-a play in so confusing a way that on the pre-London tour, in Manchester, theatregoers were seen to strike matches and stare at their programmes in a desperate attempt to see where they – or, rather, the characters on stage – were supposed to be. The show was simplified and improved for its London opening and managed to run for four months, but Noël was relieved to leave the cast to their own devices while he travelled round the Mediterranean on a fact-finding mission for Lord Louis Mountbatten – asking sailors what sort of movies they'd like to see, always provided that the Royal Navy managed to come up with enough projectors to make films on board ship a regular part of the men's Rest and Recreation.

Of all the songs in *Operette*, three stand out. One, relatively unknown, is 'Where Are the Songs We Sung?' (the ear suggests that 'Where Are the Songs We Sang?' might sound better), to which anyone over the age of 40 could and perhaps still can relate without too much difficulty:

> *Where are the songs we sung*
> *When Love in our hearts was young?*
> *Where, in the limbo of the swiftly passing years,*
> *Lie all our hopes and dreams and fears?*
> *Where have they gone – words that rang so true*
> *When Love in our hearts was new?*
> *Where in the shadows that we have to pass among,*
> *Lie those songs that we once sung?*

The second song, which became a regular stand-by in his cabaret and concert appearances ever after, was 'The Stately Homes of England'. As with 'Mad Dogs and Englishmen' this was a song that made fun of something apparently sacrosanct – the upper classes and their struggle to hang on to their country houses in an age of high income tax and death duties – while also being an affectionate salute to the subjects of the song, the very people with whom Noël had first gone to stay as an entertainer when, early in his 20s, he was still trying to escape the family boarding-house:

> *The Stately Homes of England,*
> *How beautiful they stand,*
> *To prove the upper classes*

Have still the upper hand;
Though the fact that they have to be rebuilt
And frequently mortgaged to the hilt
Is inclined to take the gilt
Off the gingerbread,
And certainly damps the fun
Of the elder son –
But still we won't be beaten,
We'll scrimp and scrape and save,
The playing fields of Eton
Have made us frightfully brave –
And though if the Van Dycks have to go
And we pawn the Bechstein Grand,
We'll stand
By the Stately Homes of England.

The third song is a typically elegiac number, even though it's about a love that has been found rather than lost:

Dearest Love,
Now that I've found you
The stars change in the sky,
Every song is new,
Every note is true,
Sorrows like the clouds go sailing by.
Here my Love,
Magic has bound you
To me – ever to be
In my heart supreme,
Dearer than my dearest dream,
The only love for me!

Operette was in one sense the latest challenge in Noël's friendly rivalry with Ivor Novello, who had followed Noël's *Cavalcade* into Drury Lane, in 1935 at the behest of the management, who were at a loss to fill the vast theatre with a show as large-scale as Noël's popular hit. Ivor's offering was *Glamorous Night*, an epic Ruritanian musical which combined romance, glamour, and a selection of hummable melodies with spectacular stage sets, lavish costumes – and a ship that sank, in full view, on stage.

Ivor's unexpected success with *Glamorous Night* (he had more or less given up composing since the First World War, at the beginning of which he had had a hit with 'Keep the Home Fires Burning') was followed by other hits at the Lane – *Careless Rapture* in 1936 and *Crest of the Wave* in 1937. Noël, who had once had a clear lead with *Bitter Sweet*, threw *Operette* into the ring, only to have it knocked out the following year by Novello's *The Dancing Years*. This surprisingly topical musical (it dealt with the rise of the Nazis and the persecution of the Jews, as well as telling a more conventional love story about a young composer and an opera singer) left Drury Lane once war broke out but, on tour and back in London at the Adelphi, was to be the most popular British musical of the 1939–45 years.

These began, of course, in September 1939, at the end of a year when Noël was working in New York, where he wrote and directed a revue, *Set to Music* (a Broadway version of *Words and Music*) and published a book of short stories, *To Step Aside*.

The war, when it came, looked as though it might put an end to Noël's entire career, as the theatres were closed down and the British public awaited the onslaught of Hitler's Luftwaffe, in an atmosphere of fear created by the topical phrase – 'the bomber will always get through'. Noël, unlike such literary figures as Christopher Isherwood and W H Auden, chose not to see the war out from the safety of America, but to return to Britain, where he was determined to contribute to the war effort in a vastly more effective way than he had done in 1918.

Initially this took the form of secret propaganda work on behalf of the government – starting in Paris. Noël found the Germans far more effective in this department than the British, who seemed mainly to rely on dropping copies of speeches by Neville Chamberlain and Lord Halifax. Regarding this policy, Noël wrote to his Intelligence handler, Sir Campbell Stuart, *If it is the policy of His Majesty's Government to bore the Germans to death, I don't believe we have quite enough time.*

But boredom was a problem for him, too, and with little visibly happening in Paris, the press (rarely the best of his friends) wondered just what Mr Coward was doing 'sauntering along the Rue Royal in naval uniform'. In fact, the report was a fabrication but, under orders not to say anything about his activities, he complied, and the idea that he was somehow having a 'soft' war stuck in people's minds.

Noël wanted to make a more substantial contribution to the war effort than this first, rather nebulous employment. He was to get his wish, and though it wasn't answered in the way he expected, the 1940s were to prove to be among the most definitive and artistically rewarding – especially on film – of his entire career.

A pretty exciting thing to be English

In 1940 Noël left Paris for New York, on a mission to assess the American attitude to the war in Europe, which was now, after almost a year, becoming considerably more intense. By the time he arrived in Washington, he realised that many American politicians even a year before Pearl Harbor saw entry into the European war as inevitable. The two opposing views, for isolation or for involvement, were summarised for him, in person, by President Roosevelt, who invited him to the White House. As in the early years of his success, however, Noël had to pay for the invitation by singing for his supper; the President demanded a rendition of 'Mad Dogs and Englishmen'. This may have been galling for Coward – he was there on behalf of the British Government, not as an entertainer – but it did at least show an affectionate interest in the English on behalf of the President of the United States.

'Mad Dogs and Englishmen' was also a favourite number of Churchill's – he had asked Noël to sing it for him at Chartwell when the two men met at the beginning of the war (before Churchill was Prime Minister) to talk about Noël's possible involvement in hostilities. And when Churchill (by then PM) and Roosevelt met on a warship, HMS *Prince of Wales*, for a conference, the two men became involved in a row about where in the song the line 'In Bangkok at twelve o'clock they foam at the mouth and run' came. Roosevelt was right, as Noël told Churchill when he related the story to him. 'England can take it' growled the Prime Minister.

In America, Noël continued to try to raise public support for the Allied cause, including the organisation of an Allied relief ball in New York on 10 May, the day that news of the German invasion of the Netherlands reached America. At the ball were two other exiles, Laurence Olivier and Vivien Leigh, then starring in a badly reviewed production of *Romeo and Juliet*, which had cost several thousand dollars of their newly earned Hollywood fortunes. *My darlings*, said Noël, *how brave of you to come!*

As the German advance continued, Noël's spymaster, Sir Campbell Stuart, was replaced by Duff Cooper, an old friend of Coward, while on a higher level Neville Chamberlain was replaced by Winston Churchill. Despite being told by Cooper that it was entirely up to him whether to return home to a war-torn Britain or not, but with the hint that he might be better employed staying in the States to drum up American support and sympathy for Britain's increasingly desperate plight, Noël decided that he wanted to be in England in her darkest hour.

The playwright and composer who had joked and mocked his way through the 1920s and 1930s was, at heart, an old-fashioned, deeply sentimental (in the best sense of the word) patriot, and, with his family and friends facing the daily danger of invasion, he wanted to be back home, in the England he so admired:

I loved its follies and apathies and curious streaks of genius; I loved standing to attention for 'God Save the King'; I loved British courage, British humour, and British understatement; I loved the justice, efficiency and even the dullness of British Colonial Administration. I loved the people – the ordinary, the extraordinary, the good, the bad, the indifferent – and what is more I belonged to that exasperating, weather-sodden little island with its uninspired cooking, its muddled thinking and its unregenerate pride, and it belonged to me whether it liked it or not. There was no escape, no getting round it, that was my personal truth and facing up to it, once and for all, I experienced a strong sense of relief.

Returning to Europe by ship, he arrived at Lisbon only to be told that a return to his office in Paris was out of the question owing to the rapid German advance, so he caught a plane for

Bordeaux, from where he took the last civilian flight out of France for five years and flew to London.

But Noël's homecoming was an anti-climax as he could find no useful war work, and he returned to America for further propaganda and more research into the American willingness to go to war. While in New York, he also oversaw his mother and Aunt Vida's evacuation to his apartment on East 52nd Street. He also saw Moss Hart, the writer/director then negotiating with Gertrude Lawrence about *Lady in the Dark*. They spoke not of the war but of the theatre – something that Noël was often quick to criticise in others, especially later in the war, as his diary entry about dinner with the ballet dancer Robert Helpmann on Tuesday 7 October 1941 shows:

> *Dined at Ivy. Conversation with Bobbie Helpmann about how difficult it is to keep the Ballet going with people being called up all the time. Thought of Poland, Holland, Czechoslovakia, Norway, Belgium, France etc., and felt it was indeed terrible not to keep the Ballet going. To do him justice, he was very good about it, but I felt there was something intrinsically wrong with the whole subject.*

Noël during his tour of Australia

Unable to find immediately practical war work in either Britain or America, Noël accepted an invitation to tour Australia and New Zealand as a guest of their respective governments, to make broadcasts and give concerts, all the time fundraising for war efforts. This he did with great success, realising that although his natural setting was in nightclubs and theatres, he was also able to entertain camps full of troops under canvas or in the open air, and he was to spend many of the remaining years of the war doing just that.

When not performing in concert or cabaret, he was writing, directing and starring in plays and films, having finally abandoned any attempts to make a more 'serious' contribution to the war effort, given that the establishment only seemed to want him as a light-hearted entertainer. As it was, his contribution to morale through his plays, films and concerts was of far greater effect than any government service would ever have been, and he was, at heart, relieved to be back in the world he knew so well and of which he would continue to prove to be (hence his nickname) The Master:

I have tried from the beginning to work constructively for the war effort and now, having been driven back to my own metier, the theatre, I cannot work myself up about it any more. This may be sheer escapism, but if I can make people laugh etc., maybe I am not doing so very badly. I only know that to sit at the side of the stage amid the old familiar sights and sounds and smells is really lovely after all this long time. The only things that matter to me at the moment are whether or not I was good in such and such a scene and if the timing was right and my make-up not too pale. This is my job, really, and will remain so through all wars and revolutions and carnage.

Back in Britain in early 1941, he had first-hand experience of the Blitz – albeit in the relative comfort of the Savoy Hotel, as another diary entry recalls: *Lunched Dorchester with Bob Menzies {the long-serving Australian premier}. He was absolutely charming. Came away comfortably reassured that I had done a really good job there.*

Had a few drinks, then went to Savoy. Pretty bad Blitz, but not so bad as Wednesday. A couple of bombs fell very near during dinner. Wall bulged a bit and door blew in. Orchestra went on playing, no one stopped eating or talking. Blitz continued. Caroll Gibbons played the piano, I sang, so did Judy Campbell and a couple of drunken Scots Canadians. On the whole, a strange and very amusing evening. People's behaviour absolutely magnificent. Much better than gallant. Wish the whole of America could really see and understand it. Thankful to God I came back. Would not have missed this experience for anything. (Saturday 19 April 1941)

This was a personal experience of the best of the British under pressure, and it confirmed both his own grace under pressure and that of his countrymen. As he was later to write in his diary for July of that year (and echoing his *Cavalcade* curtain-call speech), *It certainly is a pretty exciting thing to be English.*

This feeling of patriotism came home to him when one morning in 1941 he had gone to meet a friend off a train in Paddington. The night before, there had been a very bad Blitz, and all the glass in the station roof had been blown out. Noël said that he sat on a station bench watching Londoners scurrying about in the thin spring sunshine, magnificently unfazed by the glass, and suddenly he remembered an old London folk song which had been stolen by the Germans and shamefully turned into their National Anthem. Now, he felt, more than ever, was the time to bring it home to where it had always belonged.

> *London Pride has been handed down to us.*
> *London Pride is a flower that's free.*
> *London Pride means our own dear town to us,*
> *And our pride it for ever will be.*
> *Grey city*
> *Stubbornly implanted,*
> *Taken so for granted*
> *For a thousand years.*
> *Stay, city,*
> *Smokily enchanted,*
> *Cradle of our memories and hopes and fears.*
> *Every Blitz*
> *Your resistance*

> *Toughening,*
> *From the Ritz*
> *To the Anchor and Crown,*
> *Nothing ever could override*
> *The pride of London Town.*

While on the subject of wartime songs, 'Could You Please Oblige Us With a Bren Gun?' brilliantly recaptures the amateurish, make-do but plucky attitude among the Home Guard that was, in the 1960s, to inspire the long-running television series *Dad's Army*. Armed often only with broom handles during drill, and with barely an effective weapon between them, these squads of volunteers prepared to repel the apparently invincible German war machine in the event of an invasion – which in the early years of the war appeared imminent.

While taking a slyly satirical look at this, Coward's song also has an undertone of contempt for the lack of resources available to the Home Guard, and he was scathing, in private and in his diaries, about the parlous state of the British armed forces, thanks, in his opinion, to the blindness and complacency of those in power in the late 1930s:

> *Could you please oblige us with a Bren gun?*
> *We need it rather badly I'm afraid.*
> *Our local crossword-solver.*
> *Has an excellent revolver;*
> *But during a short*
> *Attack on a fort*
> *The trigger got mislaid.*
> *In the course of operations planned for Friday afternoon*
> *Our orders are to storm the Hippodrome;*
> *So if you can't oblige us with a Bren gun –*
> *The Home Guard might as well go home.*

When, several years later, it became clear that the Allies were going to win, Noël anticipated another daft but ineffably English reaction, after the war, to the appeasement that he believed had helped cause the conflict in the first place. The song, 'Don't Let's Be Beastly to the Germans' was initially banned by the BBC on the grounds that it was pro-German, when in fact it was intended as an exasperated warning that being too generous in defeat (in contrast to the victors' behaviour at the end of the First World War) might well lead to renewed trouble 20 years down the line. It also anticipated, by a couple of decades, the self-flagellation of the British establishment in its dealings with any foreign government:

Don't let's be beastly to the Germans
When our victory is ultimately won,
It was just those nasty Nazis who persuaded them to fight
And their Beethoven and Bach are really far worse than their bite.
Let's be meek to them –
And turn the other cheek to them
And try to bring out their latent sense of fun.
Let's give them full air parity –
And treat the rats with charity,
But don't let's be beastly to the Hun.

Don't let's be beastly to the Germans
For you can't deprive a gangster of his gun
Though they've been a little naughty to the Czechs and Poles
    and Dutch
But I don't suppose those countries really minded very much.
Let's be free with them and share the B.B.C. with them.
We mustn't prevent them basking in the sun.
Let's soften their defeat again – and build their bloody fleet again,
But don't let's be beastly to the Hun.

The year 1941 was most memorable for one of Noël's biggest hits to date – *Blithe Spirit*. This was written, while on holiday with Joyce Carey in Wales, in just six days, and was to be performed almost exactly as written – with only two lines cut and none altered in rehearsal.

In the course of Noël's writing, the role of Madame Arcati – a medium who unwittingly summons up the ghost of the first wife (Elvira) of Charles Condomine, an elegant man-about-town now married to his second wife, Ruth – Noël expanded the dotty medium into a major comic character, and she has been a favourite part for actresses of a certain age the world over ever since.

Blithe Spirit opened in London on 2 July 1941 and was an immediate hit with critics and public alike, though Graham Greene, writing in *The Spectator*, thought it 'a weary exhibition of bad taste'. The main appeal (apart from the obvious one of a drawing-room comedy brilliantly constructed and packed with amusing one-liners) was that, at a time of appalling suffering and

Constance Cummings, Kay Hammond and Rex Harrison in the film version of *Blithe Spirit*

worry about menfolk in the armed services overseas, *Blithe Spirit* gave audiences something to laugh about, while defying the ever-present Death as 'a cunning little trick, all done with mirrors' to quote Elyot in *Private Lives*.

In 1942 Noël took *Blithe Spirit* on tour, now playing the central role himself, along with his latest plays *Present Laughter* and *This Happy Breed*, productions in which his leading lady was Judy Campbell. Their tour took in a wide range of provincial theatres, many of them freezing cold during the winter. On one occasion, during a love scene, Noël's hand uncharacteristically slipped under Judy's Molyneux dress and onto her breast, which he cupped lovingly for the duration of the scene. Thinking she had finally aroused some heterosexual interest, Judy hugged him off-stage afterwards, only to be told *Thanks for letting me do that – it was the first time my hand's been warm all evening!*

The play is not only a witty ghost story, but also a sophisticated and entertaining exposé of two marriages in crisis: Charles's current one, to Ruth, and the previous one to Elvira. It also takes a less than serious view of the occult, and laughs at death as well as at the prospect of eternal life (which Noël didn't believe in) by taking the audience with him rather than openly deriding a belief that, in time of war, offered a lot of people an essential comfort.

As *The Times* suggested, this is a play that some women might find irritating – 'the denouement carries the possibly ungallant and certainly facile implication that wives present only one problem to the well-regulated masculine mind: how they are to be got rid of' – but it struck a happy chord with the theatre-going public in 1941 and has been a hit with them ever since. Of all Noël's plays it is the one most frequently performed by amateurs, and has been back in the West End professionally no less than half a dozen times since the war, most recently at the Savoy with Penelope Keith as the dotty medium (in 2005).

Of the two new plays, *This Happy Breed* was a throwback to his original South London childhood. Like *Cavalcade*, it told the story of just one family, but now the time frame was the 20 years that separated the Armistice of 1918 from the Munich crisis of 1938.

Noël was here writing of the Clapham Commoners he had always known (*I was born somewhere in the middle of the social scale, and therefore got a good view of both the upper and the lower reaches*) and a tendency in his writing to make them all overarticulate was more or less offset by the accuracy with which he depicted the changing patterns of family life through one generation.

This Happy Breed is a microcosmic impression of what England was like for one family at one time, in which action comes second to dialogue and in which the ultimate hero is England itself. The other play in this sequence of three, *Present Laughter* (originally entitled *Sweet Sorrow* and therefore always known in France as *Joyeux Chagrins*), was ostensibly at least still more autobiographical: *It is,* wrote Noël later, *a very light comedy and was written with the sensible object of providing me with a bravura part. It was an enormous success. I received excellent notices and, to my bewilderment and considerable dismay, the play was also reasonably acclaimed. This so unnerved me that I can say no more.*

Like *Hay Fever*, but written 20 years later, *Present Laughter* is a comedy about the 'theatricals' that Noël best knew and loved and cherished in his public and private lives, but this time written as a star vehicle for himself. Over the years, the play has proved to be a well-oiled and perfectly satisfactory vehicle for a wide range of disparate other actors, from Nigel Patrick and Peter O'Toole to Tom Conti and Albert Finney.

Its central character, Gary Essendine, is in many ways the world-weary middle-aged projection of the dilettante, debonair persona first accorded to Coward by the media after the success of *The Vortex* back in 1924. He is a witty, tiresome, self-obsessed, silk-dressing-gowned figure who struts through the play like an educated peacock. But at the end of the first act, there is a revealing moment when Essendine, through whom can be very loudly heard the voice of his creator and first player, is called upon to give some advice to an importunate young playwright of the next generation: 'To begin with, your play is not a play at all. It is a meaningless jumble of adolescent, pseudo-intellectual poppycock. It bears no relation to the theatre or to life or to anything . . . If you wish to be a playwright, you just leave the theatre of tomorrow to take care of itself. Go and get yourself a job as a butler in a repertory company, if they'll have you. Learn from the ground up how plays are constructed, and what is actable and what isn't. Then sit down and write at least twenty plays, one after the other, and if you can manage to get the twenty-first produced for a Sunday-night performance, you'll be damned lucky.'

A potent mixture of self-exposure and self-celebration, was Noël's own verdict on Gary as late as 1972, and somewhere in *Present Laughter* there is indeed a great deal of truth, not only about Coward in mid-career, but also about the group of friends, secretaries, managers and lovers which had by now grouped itself around his star presence. In one sense, no play he ever wrote was more autobiographical, but in another sense, the conjuring trick is still intact. Gary is not really Noël, merely a reflection of him through a series of fairground distorting mirrors. Now you see him, now you don't, and if the play is about anything very philosophical, it is surely about the price of fame and the cost of charm.

Despite the effects of the war, Noël's private life was by now beginning to stabilise; early and brief homosexual affairs had given way to longer relationships with the theatre manager Jack Wilson, then the actor Alan Webb, and soon after the war the singer Graham Payn, who was to stay with him until the very end of his life. There was also his faithful secretary Lorn Loraine, and a remarkable valet-turned-personal-assistant, Cole Lesley, who, like Graham, was also to be at Noël's deathbed in Jamaica more than 30 years after first joining his service.

Added to that inner circle were the designer Gladys Calthrop, the actress Joyce Carey and much later Joan Hirst, who came in to assist Lorn and took over her work in the last years of Noël's life and until her own death in the 1990s.

Unlike Novello's court, who were all fundamentally players in his company, the group that formed itself around Noël in these years came from a wide variety of backgrounds and pursued very different careers within the broad spectrum of theatre. But what they had in common was a near-lifelong devotion to Noël, a determination to keep his private life out of the papers, and an equal determination to defend him when (increasingly in the post-war years) he was to come under attack, either for being a tax exile or hopelessly out of touch with so-called modern theatre. Now and forever they were his cheerleaders, and he was eternally grateful for their support in sometimes critical conditions.

Noël's cinema career also took off in 1941, when he wrote, produced and co-directed, with David Lean, *In Which We Serve*, his tribute to the Royal Navy in general and to the officers and crew

Noël paid homage to the wartime Royal Navy in the film *In Which We Serve*

of HMS *Kelly*, the ship sunk in action under the command of his old friend Lord Louis Mountbatten.

In Which We Serve may have been a morale-boosting film about the gallantry of the Royal Navy, but senior elements of the navy were less than enthusiastic about the idea of Noël Coward playing the captain of a warship, one moreover sent to the bottom of the sea, and it took the full force of Louis Mountbatten's determination (not to mention his vanity) and royal contacts to get the film made, with – eventually – the full cooperation of the naval authorities.

Noël was delighted with the results, writing to his mother that *it will be the best thing I have ever done . . . a naval* Cavalcade *that is absolutely right for this time.* Shooting started on 5 February 1942 and lasted for some 20 weeks, during which the King, Queen and Princesses visited the set and voiced their approval and support. This was, in many ways, the apotheosis of Noël's social networking in the 1920s and 1930s: the King was the trump card that he was able to play in all the fraught offscreen negotiations with the initially reluctant authorities in the course of writing and making the film.

The result was an epic, deeply moving, patriotic and yet in many ways superbly understated film that was, as he had predicted to his mother, ideal for its time. As Captain Kinross, Noël threw off any traces of the green room and metamorphosed into someone who was every inch an officer and gentleman, and his speech to the crew of HMS *Torrin* was a latter-day variation on Henry V's on the eve of Agincourt – quieter, less showy, yet every bit as effective on the audience.

In Which We Serve was released at the end of 1942, a couple of months after another but very different Coward film, *We Were Dancing* (starring Norma Shearer and Melvyn Douglas), an MGM version of his play of the same name from *Tonight at 8.30.* That film was undistinguished, but *In Which We Serve* raised Noël's stock among the general public, and was immediately recognised as a wartime classic. Had he not had already had a dispute with the Inland Revenue over his American earnings (all his life he seemed dogged with tax troubles of one sort or another), *In Which We Serve* might have been as much a passport to a knighthood as the film of *Henry V* was to prove for Laurence Olivier.

Both films caught the public's imagination, with their stories of defiance in the face of the enemy, an enemy which in *Henry V* came in overwhelming numbers. *In Which We Serve* didn't have the benefit of Shakespeare's extraordinarily potent language, but it did have the immediacy of being about the current war, based on fact and with an equally stirring call to arms.

Its quality of clenched courage in adversity was exactly right for the period, as was the sense of a beleaguered Britain pluckily fighting on, alone, against the odds – something that was mythologised as soon as France fell in May 1940, and has continued to be the received wisdom ever since. In fact, of course, Britain was a Great Power, with an enormous Empire, naval bases that controlled every important sea lane on the planet, and a Royal Navy that was (until the American shipbuilding programme got into top gear halfway through the war) easily the most powerful navy in the world.

Britain was also allied to another Great Power, France, whose army had been the largest and most highly regarded in Europe until it fell apart under Hitler's *blitzkrieg* in 1940, and, as it turned out, for all its deservedly formidable reputation from Guernica onwards, the Luftwaffe was no match for the Royal Air Force. Which makes a nonsense of the myth of Britain as a small but plucky nation somehow scratching together an amateur response to a vastly larger and infinitely more professional opponent.

In Which We Serve was itself a reminder of the professionalism and remarkably consistent record of the Royal Navy for winning battles, let alone wars, since the early 18th century, and it helped restore a sense of pride and achievement to a cinema-going public who, until El Alamein (also in 1942) had had to cope with endless newsreel stories of defeats and withdrawals by British armies, from North Africa to Singapore.

The year after the release of *In Which We Serve*, Noël returned to London (to the Theatre Royal, Haymarket), to star in *Present Laughter* and *This Happy Breed*, also producing a film version of the latter.

He also found time to tour the Middle East, entertaining the troops who, since El Alamein, were at long last winning the war against the German and Italian armies, with whom they had been locked in combat in the sands of North Africa. His experiences were published the following year in a book, *Middle East Diary*.

The last full year of the war, 1944, was spent largely on tour, entertaining troops in South Africa, India, Burma and – after the D-Day landings – in France. It was a sign of the government's awareness of the importance of theatrical entertainment to the morale of the troops in the field that troupes of actors and entertainers were sent over to Normandy remarkably soon after the invasion. Ivor Novello's new tune, 'We'll Gather Lilacs' was heard by battlefield troops in France months before it was first played to theatre-goers back home, where it was the hit number in Novello's 1945 musical, *Perchance to Dream*.

For all that it was to be spent in various parts of the British Empire, 1944 began, for Noël, in New York, where it inspired one of his less well-known poems – 'Happy New Year'. This came to him as he considered the contrast between the party he was attending and the fate that had befallen so many young men and was lurking in wait for many more:

> *'Happy New Year' the fifth year of the war.*
> *'To Victory' – 'To Nineteen Forty-four'*
> *'To all our fighting men' 'To their release*
> *From carnage' – 'To a world at last at peace'*

These were the words we said. The glib, confused
Hopelessly hopeful phrases that we used.
Then we had more champagne – somebody sang
Supper was served – outside we heard a gang
Of revellers gaily carousing by
Blowing their foolish squeakers at the sky.
'Happy New Year' – Happy New Year for whom?
How many people in that scented room?
How many people in that drunken crew
Squealing and swaying down Fifth Avenue
Thought for a moment; felt the faintest doubt;
Wondered what they were being gay about?
Here in New York, with shrill conviviality
Toasting their lack of contact with reality
Lifting my glass, I sadly bowed my head
Silently to congratulate the Dead.

Another of his wartime poems, and probably his best, is about the young men who made up the bomber crews that set off from airfields in England to bomb German cities, ports and industrial targets, in an air campaign that was to cost, in the course of the war, some 50,000 lives. It is called 'Lie in the Dark and Listen':

Lie in the dark and listen,
It's clear tonight so they're flying high
Hundreds of them, thousands perhaps,
Riding the icy, moonlight sky.
Men, material, bombs and maps
Altimeters and guns and charts
Coffee, sandwiches, fleece-lined boots
Bones and muscles and minds and hearts
English saplings with English roots
Deep in the earth they've left below

Lie in the dark and let them go
Lie in the dark and listen.

Lie in the dark and listen
They're going over in waves and waves
High above villages, hills and streams
Country churches and little graves
And little citizens' worried dreams.
Very soon they'll have reached the sea
And far below them will lie the bays
And coves and sands where they used to be
Taken for summer holidays.
Lie in the dark and let them go
Lie in the dark and listen.

Lie in the dark and listen
City magnates and steel contractors,
Factory workers and politicians
Soft, hysterical little actors
Ballet dancers, 'Reserved' musicians,
Safe in your warm, civilian beds.
Count your profits and count your sheep
Life is flying above your heads
Just turn over and try to sleep.
Lie in the dark and let them go
Theirs is a world you'll never know
Lie in the dark and listen.

The poem led to a predictably irate outcry from those in the
'reserved' professions, many of whom were eager to remark
that Noël's own war service had not often been in the line of
direct fire. At least 1944 saw, for all its slaughter – from the
beaches of Normandy to the South Pacific – the beginning of

the liberation of Europe and the probability of defeat for Nazi Germany and its allies.

That promise came increasingly close to fruition in 1945, despite the best efforts of Hitler's 'secret weapons' – the V1s and V2s that wreaked havoc on a civilian population no longer suffering the mass German bomber raids that had characterised the early years of the war. For Noël, 1945 was divided between the theatre and the cinema.

He wrote *Sigh No More* at the beginning of the year, and it was staged at the Piccadilly Theatre in London (in August 1945) following a Manchester try-out. Writing later, he described the show's genesis, as he went to Cornwall to concentrate on the project: *The planning was then only tentative because although it was generally assumed that the war would end within a few months, this was by no means certain, and if it didn't end I knew that I should have to be up and away again. At all events, I had thought of a good title,* Sigh No More, *which later, I regret to say, turned out to be the best part of the revue.*

His somewhat negative attitude to the show was reflected in his diary entry for 23 February 1946, when he wrote about the last night of its run: *Last night of* Sigh No More. *I watched it and, apart from 'Matelot', said goodbye to it without a pang.*

While it wasn't his greatest success, it did nonetheless contain some very good songs, including the title number:

> *Sigh no more, sigh no more.*
> *Grey clouds of sorrow fill the sky no more.*
> *Cry no more,*
> *Sigh no more*
> *Those little deaths at parting,*
> *New life and new love are starting,*
> *Sing again, sing again,*
> *The winter's over and its spring again.*

> *Joy is your Troubadour,*
> *Sweet and beguiling ladies, sigh no more,*
> *Sigh no more,*
> *Sweet and beguiling ladies, sigh no more.*

A comic number was 'I Wonder What Happened to Him' in which one of Noël's favourite targets, the English – in this case in the last years of the British Raj in India – once again appeared on stage in the form of a song:

> *Whatever became of old Shelley?*
> *Is it true that young Briggs was cashiered*
> *For riding quite nude on a push-bike through Delhi*
> *The day the new Viceroy appeared?*
> *Have you had any word*
> *Of that bloke in the 'Third',*
> *Was it Southerby, Sedgwick or Slim?*
> *They had him thrown out of the club in Bombay*
> *For, apart from his mess bills exceeding his pay,*
> *He took to pig-sticking in quite the wrong way.*
> *I wonder what happened to him?*

In his usual way, Noël mixed comedy with pathos; one song 'Matelot', was about a sailor whose loved ones anxiously await his return – an experience that millions of people who'd had relatives in the wartime Royal and merchant navies could instantly recognise:

> *Matelot, Matelot,*
> *Where you go my thoughts go with you,*
> *Matelot, Matelot,*
> *When you go down to the sea*
> *As you gaze from afar*
> *On the evening star*

Wherever you may roam,
You will remember the light
Through the winter night
That guides you safely home.
Though you find
Womenkind
To be frail,
One love cannot fail, my son,
Till our days are done,
Matelot, Matelot,
Where you go
My thoughts go with you,
Matelot, Matelot,
When you go down to the sea.

'Matelot' was written for Graham Payn, Coward's partner, a gifted singer and dancer who sometimes found that the pressure of Coward's ambitions for him were inclined through nobody's fault to hinder rather than help his career. Noël was an excellent child prodigy but perhaps a less secure stage godfather.

In this same victory year, Margaret Rutherford repeated her stage success in the film version of *Blithe Spirit*, while *Still Life*, one of the plays in *Tonight at 8.30* was turned into what was to become one of the most popular and critically successful British films ever made, *Brief Encounter*.

Brief Encounter starred Celia Johnson as a middle-class house-wife, with a son and a daughter and a nice but dull husband. At the railway station on her 'afternoon out shopping' in a neigh-bouring town (the film was supposedly set in the Midlands but is clearly set – spiritually if not physically – in the Home Counties), she gets a piece of grit in her eye, and has it removed by a gallant and equally middle-aged doctor, played by Trevor Howard. The two meet again, by chance, and fall in love.

Celia Johnson and Trevor Howard in *Brief Encounter*, the classic film adaptation of Coward's play *Still Life*

One of the greatest romantic films ever made, it has no sex scenes, yet the fact that their passion is understated, indeed unillustrated, while couched in simple, undramatic language and gestures (Celia's inner torment is expressed by her sitting on a park bench, at night, in the rain, smoking, while her voiceover narrating the film acknowledges that her husband hates women smoking in public) adds enormously to its emotional impact on the viewer.

There is also a strong period charm – steam trains, Boots libraries, an organist at the cinema, musicians at the local restaurant. Not to mention the very idea that women shouldn't smoke in public, unlike men. And, of course, there's Celia Johnson's extraordinarily clipped voice. Far from alienating modern audiences, this now seems wistfully charming and of its curiously clenched period, though when the film was first released it led to calls of derision from some working-class cinemagoers, despite Johnson's huge, hurt eyes which would surely melt anyone's heart.

The film's success, at the time of its first immediately post-war release, was obviously not based on nostalgia – this was very much a contemporary piece, after all – but on the fact that it was dealing with peacetime, after years of films about the war. Adultery might be heartbreaking, even when unconsummated, but at least it was part of 'normal' life.

Even before peace finally arrived (which it only did, in the Far East, with the dropping of the two atom bombs on Hiroshima and Nagasaki), the public had voted for a new form of peacetime society, when, in the 1945 general election, it returned a Labour government. Unsurprisingly, Noël was firmly on Churchill's side, and he was appalled when Labour not only won, but by a landslide:

A highly dramatic day in our 'Turbulent Island Story'. The Labour Government is sweeping in on an overwhelming majority . . . It is appalling to think that our Allies and enemies can see us chuck out the man who has led us so magnificently through these horrible years . . . This certainly gives a salutary lesson to those who set too much store by public acclaim or the power of the press. Whatever government rules us for the next few years will have a tough assignment, and it may not be a bad idea for the Labour boys to hold the baby. I always felt that England would be bloody uncomfortable during the immediate post-war period, and it is now almost a certainty that it will be so.

The same sentiments could be as easily summed up in one of his songs from this period time, 'There Are Bad Times Just Around the Corner':

There are bad times just around the corner
And the outlook's absolutely vile,
You can take this from us
That when they atom bomb us
We are NOT going to tighten our belts and smile, smile, smile

We are in such a mess
It couldn't matter less
If a world revolution is just ahead,
We'd better all learn the lyrics of the old 'Red Flag'
And wait until we drop down dead.
A likely story
Land of Hope and Glory,
Wait until we drop down dead.

The later 1940s were indeed to prove to be a tough time ('Mr Coward has survived the war' wrote the critic Cyril Connolly, 'now we wait to see if he can survive the peace.') and were to be remembered as the Austerity years. Noël's attitude to Attlee's government was to remain pretty much that of another right-wing writer, Evelyn Waugh, who insisted on referring to the Labour Government as an Enemy Occupation.

Surviving the peace

In yet another attempt to fend off the invasion of the Broadway musical, and incidentally to recapture the glamour and charm of the pre-war years, Noël decided on a major musical, *Pacific 1860*, at the Theatre Royal, Drury Lane. That Drury Lane had been, from 1935, the theatre most closely identified in the public mind with Ivor Novello and his series of large-scale romantic musicals, was surely no coincidence. If Ivor had usurped Noël's place at the head of the British musical theatre, what better way to re-establish his claim to that title than getting back into the Lane with a hit musical of his own?

Gladys Calthrop and Noël at a rehearsal of *Pacific 1860*

Unfortunately, *Pacific 1860* proved to be a costly failure, offering the critics a target for savage attack and leading to a breach between Noël and his leading lady, Mary Martin, that was to last the better part of a decade. They finally resumed their friendship with a successful joint concert in New York, albeit on television rather than in the theatre.

Part of the problem had been the sheer level of expectation – this was the show that was re-opening London's grandest theatre, whose last major musical, in 1939, Novello's *The Dancing Years*, had proved to be a massive hit. Critics naturally made a comparison between the two – one damned *Pacific 1860* with faint praise, saying it was 'faintly reminiscent of Ivor Novello' – and although advance sales had been very good, a combination of tepid reviews for an unashamedly but unwisely nostalgic romance, and an appallingly cold winter, meant that the show only lasted four months, the last two being, according to Noël, *more of a convulsive stagger than a run*.

But the real trouble lay in rehearsal: Drury Lane needed a major refit after its wartime use as the headquarters of ENSA, the armed services' entertainment unit, but post-war restrictions meant that all materials for the rebuild were limited and rationed, added to which in a bitterly cold winter (with the cast dressed for a South Sea island) the theatre's heating system had packed up. Backstage conditions were, to put it mildly, less than perfect.

But there were still a couple of good numbers – and, ironically for a romance, they were the comic relief. 'Uncle Harry' was an entertaining account of man who, like a latter-day HMS *Bounty* mutineer, found himself overwhelmed by the charms of the South Pacific:

> *Poor Uncle Harry*
> *Wanted to be a missionary*
> *So he took a ship and sailed away.*
> *This visionary,*
> *Hotly pursued by dear Aunt Mary,*

Found a South Sea Isle on which to stay.
The natives greeted them kindly and invited them to dine
On yams and clams and human hams and vintage coconut wine,
The taste of which was filthy but the after-effects divine.
Poor Uncle Harry
Got a bit gay and longed to tarry.
This, Aunt Mary couldn't quite allow,
She lectured him severely on a number of church affairs
But when she'd gone to bed he made a get-away down the stairs,
For he longed to find the answer to a few of the maiden's prayers.
Uncle Harry's not a missionary now.

Another comic song, was 'Alice Is At It Again', which Mary
Martin refused to sing as she considered it vulgar:

The smiles between Noël and Mary Martin in *Pacific 1860* were shortlived

Over the field and along the lane
Gentle Alice would love to stray,
When it came to the end of the day,
She would wander away unheeding,
Dreaming her innocent dreams she strolled
Quite unaffected by heat or cold,
Frequently freckled or soaked with rain,
Alice was out in the lane.
Whom she met there
Every day there
Was a question answered by none,
But she'd stay there
Till whatever she did was undoubtedly done.
Over the field and along the lane
When her parents had called in vain,
Sadly, sorrowfully, they'd complain,
'Alice is at it again'.

Having endured a critical mauling with an all-new musical, Noël decided in 1947 to revive an old favourite, *Present Laughter*, in which he starred as Gary Essendine, the self-assured playwright, at the Theatre Royal, Haymarket.

He also directed a revival of *Tonight at 8.30*, which toured the United States with Gertrude Lawrence and Graham Payn and, when Graham was ill, played his last-ever performances with Gertie for two or three nights in San Francisco. At the same time his *Point Valaine* was produced in London to a muted reception from audiences and critics alike.

Broadway meanwhile welcomed back a revival of *Private Lives*, and continental Europe began a sustained post-war enthusiasm for Coward with a Belgian production of *Joyeux Chagrins* (*Present Laughter*) in Brussels, in which Noël played the character now known as Max Aramont in fluent French.

Graham Payn, Gertrude Lawrence and Noël rehearse a dance routine for *Tonight at 8.30*

The year 1949 was relatively quiet, with another film drawn from the *Tonight at 8.30* sequence, *The Astonished Heart*, in which he also starred as the doomed, love-tortured psychiatrist, a role from which he had fired his sometime lover Michael Redgrave early in the shooting. But the film was not a success, while by contrast his old friend and friendly rival, Ivor Novello, had his biggest hit, with a defiantly Ruritanian musical in which Ivor co-starred with Vanessa Lee: *King's Rhapsody*. As Noël wrote in his diary:

Got home from Pinewood in time to go with Graham to Ivor's first night – King's Rhapsody. *It was a violently glamorous evening. The show was much better than anything he has done before. It had a few embarrassing moments and was, as usual, too long, but Zena Dare was excellent and Vanessa Lee absolutely enchanting; a lovely voice, very good looks and can act. Terrific ovation at the end. We dined at the Ivy and Rebecca West joined us . . .* (Thursday 15 September 1949)

The years of relative failure (other than revivals) that followed the war were in a sense the theatrical equivalent of the decline that Noël's friend Winston Churchill had undergone, but Noël, like Churchill, was to have a new lease of life in the 1950s and, unlike Winston, was to embrace the new technology (television) and a wholly new career as television entertainer and cabaret star in the New World.

Future indefinite

Having had a few years to lick his wounds, Noël started the new decade with a new musical offering – *Ace of Clubs*, which played at the Cambridge Theatre. A Soho *Guys and Dolls*, it was largely set in a nightclub, and with its Bohemian collection of sailors, gangsters and chorus girls it was intriguingly different from any of his previous work, a defiantly transatlantic attempt to move into the second half of the 20th century. However, it included one classic Coward number – 'Sail Away' – with its lilting, haunting tune and lyrics that blended the gently elegiac with a quiet defiance in a way that was typically Noël. The score also included the much more upbeat and modern 'I Like America' which, given that America had kept him in work at a time when many British critics seemed to think he was a spent theatrical force, was an entirely understandable title. It was also, given his future success in the States in cabaret and on television, strangely prophetic:

> *I like America,*
> *I have played around*
> *Every slappy-happy hunting ground*
> *But I find America – okay.*
> *I've been about a bit*
> *But I must admit*
> *That I didn't know the half of it*
> *Till I hit the USA.*
> *No likely lass*
> *In Boston, Mass,*

From passion will recoil.
In Dallas, Tex.
They talk of sex
But only think of oil.
New Jersey dames
Go up in flames
If someone mentions – bed.
In Chicago, Illinois
Any girl who meets a boy
Giggles and shoots him dead!
But I like America
Its Society
Offers infinite variety
And come what may
I shall return some day
To the good old U.S.A.

Noël's cabaret career was kick-started in the following year, 1951, when he appeared at the Café de Paris, and proved to be a brilliant solo (plus pianist Norman Hackforth) performer. Hackforth had of course been his pianist on some of the wartime troop concert tours which were the roots of his cabaret career, and the two men met again when Hackforth was accompanying another old friend, Marlene Dietrich, in cabaret at the Café. Noël chanced to ask with genuine diffidence whether they thought he might risk a similar solo season in cabaret, and so enthusiastic were they that he soon set about preparing a programme of his songs. On this musical front, he also wrote a few new songs for *The Lyric Revue*, but more importantly he returned to the stage with *Relative Values*, which he wrote and directed at the Savoy.

This was to revive his reputation as a writer of social comedies, and starred Gladys Cooper, his friend of some 30 years but with whom, amazingly, he had never worked before. Gladys and Noël had different views on the desirability of knowing the script off by heart at the start of rehearsals: 'It is ridiculous,' she commented to a friend during a break from a fraught rehearsal, knowing Coward to be in earshot. 'Noël expects me to be word-perfect at the first rehearsal.' Noël picked up the challenge: *It is not the first rehearsal I worry about, so much as the first night.* Michael Relph designed *Relative Values* rather than Gladys Calthrop, who was fading gently from Noël's professional life, if not his personal one.

Noël and Marlene Dietrich

That same year, 1951, also saw the death of Ivor Novello, whose last show, *Gay's the Word*, had premiered in London (at the Saville, now a cinema, at the unfashionable end of Shaftesbury Avenue) in February. It had been written as a favour for Cicely Courtneidge, whose career it revived, giving her a theme song 'Vitality' into the bargain. Ivor died not long after the opening night, in the early hours of 5 March, and the news was a huge blow to Noël.

Much though he was to miss him, his sadness at Ivor's death didn't get in the way of Noël's critical faculties when he eventually made it to *Gay's the Word*, though he had the good grace to record in his diary the musical's popularity:

The best in the theatre in the afternoon – Waters of the Moon – *and the worst in the theatre in the evening* Gay's the Word. *The former flawlessly played and directed, the latter stinking with bad taste and the intermixed vulgarity of Ivor and Alan Melville. Cicely Courtneidge a miracle of vitality and hard work but, oh dear, with that horrible stuff to do. It was rapturously received by a packed house.* (Wednesday 13 June 1951)

Novello and Coward had been friends and rivals for over 30 years, both claiming to enjoy each other's success, and dismissing any notion of rivalry as at worst a creation of the press, or at best a result of over-enthusiastic friends and admirers trying to talk up one's achievements at the expense of the other.

There was, however, more than a hint of truth in the belief that each wanted (however amiably) to outdo the other. Noël had one hit at Drury Lane with *Cavalcade*, so Ivor jumped at the chance of having an epic of his own – the musical *Glamorous Night* (1935) – and went on to have several more there: *Careless Rapture* (1936), *Crest of the Wave* (1937) and *The Dancing Years* (1939) – as well as an ill-fated production of *Henry V* in 1938.

Similarly, it can't have been a coincidence that Ivor chose to stage his wartime musical *Arc De Triomphe* (with Mary Ellis) at the Phoenix in 1943, given that this was where Noël had performed *Private Lives*, back in 1930. Unlike *Private Lives*, however, *Arc De Triomphe* was a rare Novello flop – it can't be just a coincidence that this was the only one of his stage musicals in which he didn't star.

For all the variety and in some cases modernity of his music, Novello never really escaped the Edwardian operettas of his teenage years (he watched *The Merry Widow* 27 times), whereas Noël epitomised the cynical view of the century that he characterised in his 'Twentieth Century Blues'. Ivor was a prolific and popular playwright (and matinee idol) throughout the 1920s and the 1930s, but Noël was a far wittier and technically more accomplished playwright who carried on practising his craft whatever other art forms – from the cinema to concert parties – attracted his attention.

Their rivalry was brought to an untimely end by Ivor's early death (he was 58 when he died in 1951), whereas Noël survived well into the television and LP-record age. Had Novello (who shortly before his death was already recreating himself with the far lighter and more modern *Gay's the Word*) carried on working, and lived into the era of television documentaries and interviews, let alone appearing in the sort of cameo roles in films that Noël so enjoyed (notably as Mr Bridger in *The Italian Job* in 1968), then Novello might be as well known as Coward today.

As it is, Noël's reputation is still strong, and he remains in the public eye, while Ivor (apart from appearing, thanks to Julian Fellowes, in the Oscar-winning *Gosford Park*) has been airbrushed out of British popular culture. Which makes all the more poignant the anecdote about Noël's arriving at the stage door of one of his shows. On being stopped by a new (and surprisingly uninformed) stage doorkeeper, Noël announced, furiously that *I not only wrote this show, I directed it and am starring in it, too!,* whereupon the doorkeeper gave him a look of withering contempt, removed the cigarette from his lower lip and said 'Right little Ivor Novello, aren't we?'

Later that year Noël appeared in a star-studded charity gala at the London Coliseum to commemorate Ivor's career, but his own career naturally went on, and in 1952 he wrote and directed *Quadrille*, which was staged at one of his favourite London theatres, the Phoenix, the one he had opened with *Private Lives* more than 20 years earlier.

Quadrille was written as a vehicle for the Lunts, who opened it in London in September, six days after Noël heard of the sudden death of Gertrude Lawrence: *We first worked together as child actors in the Playhouse Theatre, Liverpool, in 1912; since then, whether we have been acting together or not, we have been integrally part of each other's lives . . . I wish so very deeply that I could have seen her just once more playing in a play of mine, for no one I have ever known, however brilliant and however gifted, has contributed quite what she contributed to my work. Her quality was, to me, unique and her magic imperishable.*

Noël hoofs it up with Kay Kendal, Joyce Grenfell and Margaret Leighton at the London Palladium. 1951

The Lunts were reportedly irritated by this tribute, which was uncharacteristically churlish of them – Gertie's relationship with Noël was unique, and in a very real sense he never recovered from her death, which is why some 30 years later I was keen to write my *Noël and Gertie*, which plays on around the world as a reminder of their romantic, odd-couple alliance.

The critics were less than keen on *Quadrille*, with Kenneth Tynan (writing in the *Evening Standard*), though liking the Lunts, being notably less than overawed by the quality of Noël's writing: 'alas, everything is said twice over, and what was meant for a gracious sparkle ends up as a condescending wink . . . Under the weight of the lines, the plot collapses, and we are left only with negative virtues . . . The play is not snobbish, it is not vulgar, nor is it without style; but it is also not the pure fantastic Coward at whose invention we used to chuckle long after the curtain had dropped'.

However, the public thought differently, as Noël recalled: Quadrille . . . *is a romantic Victorian comedy which the critics detested and the public liked enough to fill the Phoenix Theatre for a year. It has, to my unbiased mind, a great deal to recommend it . . . in addition to {the Lunt's} ineffable contribution, the décor and dresses were designed with exquisite colour and taste by Cecil Beaton. In addition even to these matchless attributes it has in it some evocative and well written scenes, notably the 'Railway' speech in Act Three.*

Also in 1952 Noël was to contribute songs to *The Globe Revue*; he oversaw the film *Meet Me Tonight* (still three more plays from *Tonight at 8.30*, virtually all nine of which had now been transferred to the screen) and had his second stint at the Café de Paris.

This was repeated with a third engagement there in 1953, Coronation year. He was swept up in the fervour that gripped London, securing a seat in a grandstand outside Buckingham Palace. Looking down from there on the grand procession up the Mall, Noël was asked the identity of the little man travelling in an open coach with the vast Queen Salote of Tonga. *I think,* murmured Noël, *that must be her lunch*. It was also the Coronation that gave a huge and much-needed boost to the sales (and viewing) of television sets, so the occasion was to be, ultimately, a very profitable one for him as well as an enjoyably romantic combination of pomp and circumstance.

Queen Salote of Tonga in the Coronation procession, her 'lunch,' the Sultan of Kalimantaan, is hidden behind the coachman

To celebrate the Coronation and an unusually Royalist summer, Noël played King Carl Magnus in George Bernard Shaw's *The Apple Cart*, a play about a monarch who gets politically involved, clashes with his ministers and then amazingly abdicates, but instead of sailing off into a life of well-heeled boredom overseas (like the Duke of Windsor) chooses to stay – and run for Parliament as a commoner.

In 1954 Noël had another attempt at writing a major, old-fashioned, romantic musical: *After the Ball*. This was to prove a disastrous lesson in the inadvisability of constructing a show based on what ought to be sound commercial building-bricks. Construction of a musical on the grounds that the various components have all been successful in other contexts is almost bound to lead to trouble, but in Noël's mind his own reputation, allied to that of Oscar Wilde – one of the few public figures with as strong a reputation as him for wit, suavity and charm – should have resulted in a hit. Noël should have realised that the rest of the world might not prove to be Wilde about Oscar when he himself found the man's plays heavy going, as a diary entry reveals: *Am reading more of Oscar Wilde. What a tiresome, affected sod.* (Sunday 14 July 1946)

After the Ball was based on Wilde's *Lady Windermere's Fan*, and it also starred, in lead roles, two of Ivor Novello's most popular female stars: Mary Ellis and Vanessa Lee. Surely fusion, on stage, of Wilde, Coward and Novello – all of them vastly successful in their own right – in a musical starring two of Ivor's most bankable leading ladies, was bound to be a hit?

Not in fact: Noël had hired Mary Ellis without auditioning her, even though it had been nearly 15 years since her last hit – *The Dancing Years*, in 1939. Her voice was no longer up to standard, her part (and songs) had to be rewritten or cut to accommodate this unpalatable fact, and the result was an unbalanced musical that was a shadow of what it could have been. Neither Coward nor Wilde, fish nor fowl, the show ended up as an unhappy hybrid and its problems of both book and score were made all too clear by a 2004 off-Broadway revival in New York.

Noël had a costly and embarrassing failure on his hands and, three years after Novello's death, the large-scale, glamorous British musical set in aristocratic society finally died.

Mary Ellis was to survive this disaster, partly because she didn't really need the money a stage success would have brought, and partly because she had already demonstrated that whatever might have happened to her voice, she could still act, having originated the role of frustrated and vicious teacher's wife Millie Crocker-Harris in Terence Rattigan's public school drama *The Browning Version*. She was to live for nearly another 50 years, dying in January 2003, officially aged 102 but actually 104. She lived in a flat in Eaton Square, across the landing from where another great actress, Vivien Leigh, lived and (in 1967) died of TB.

The failure of *After the Ball* was a disappointment, although this wasn't an entirely wasted year for Noël, as a fourth season at the Café de Paris showed that, whatever his leading ladies' faults, he could still hack it very well on his own and was indeed increasingly preferring his own company to having to deal with recalcitrant actors in rehearsal. It was here that he was able to thank Marlene Dietrich, whose cabaret career had inspired his own, with this tribute as he introduced her to the packed audience:

The best of friends, Noël and Marlene Dietrich, at a piano in the Dorchester Hotel

We know God made trees
And the birds and the bees
And the seas for the fishes to swim in
We are also aware
That he has quite a flair
For creating exceptional women.
When Eve said to Adam
'Start calling me Madam'
The world became far more exciting
Which turns to confusion
The modern delusion
That sex is a question of lighting.
For female allure
Whether pure or impure
Has seldom reported a failure
As I know and you know
From Venus and Juno
Right down to La Dame aux Camélias.
This glamour, it seems,
Is the substance of dreams
To the most imperceptive perceiver
The Serpent of Nile
Could achieve with a smile
Far quicker results than Geneva.
Though we all might enjoy
Seeing Helen of Troy
As a gay, cabaret entertainer
I doubt that she could
Be one quarter as good
As our legendary, lovely Marlene.

This was an introduction to one leading lady, but he had to say
goodbye to the woman who had brought him into the world,

launched his career, and supported his every venture, when his mother died at the end of June 1954. He confided his feelings to his diary:

Mother died yesterday at a quarter to two . . . She was ninety-one years old and I was with her close, close, close until her last breath . . . Owing to my inability to accept any of the comforting religious fantasies about the hereafter, I have no spurious hopes that we shall meet again on some distant elysian shore. I know that it is over. Fifty-four years of love and tenderness and crossness and devotion and unswerving loyalty. Without her I could only have achieved a quarter of what I have achieved, not only in terms of success and career, but in terms of personal happiness. We have quarrelled, often violently, over the years, but she has never stood between me and my life, never tried to hold me too tightly, always let me go free. For a woman with her strength of character this was truly remarkable. She was gay, even to the last I believe, gallant certainly. There was no fear in her except for me. She was a great woman to whom I owe the whole of my life. I shall never be without her in my deep mind, but I shall never see her again. Goodbye, my darling. (Thursday 1 July 1954)

Quadrille transferred to New York, and he published *Future Indefinite*, his second volume of autobiography, in which, as with the first volume, he revealed a lot about the backstage process involved in staging a play, but virtually nothing about the backstage reality behind his carefully crafted public persona; nor, as usual, did he reveal anything at all about his homosexuality. Like his diaries, which in any case were only published after his death, his autobiographies are models of reticence and sexual discretion but for all that, hugely enjoyable anthologies of literary and dramatic criticism and travel journalism.

Meanwhile in America, and specifically in Las Vegas, his cabaret career was taking off not just because of his skills as a songwriter and the expertly effortless way he put his own songs across, but because he epitomised Old World charm for the New World audiences, for many of whom he was the next best thing to

America loved Noël Coward. Jane Powell and Zsa Zsa Gabor prove it in Las Vegas. 1955

having royalty on stage. He took a characteristically wry and shrewd view of those who so profitably employed him, as this diary entry shows:

The gangsters who run the places in Vegas are all urbane and charming. I had a feeling that if I opened a rival casino I would be battered to death with the utmost efficiency and despatch, but if I remained on my own ground as a most highly paid entertainer then I could trust them all the way . . . Their morals are bizarre in the extreme. They are generous, mother-worshippers, sentimental and capable of much kindness. They are also ruthless, cruel, violent and devoid of scruples. (Friday 3 December 1954)

If the early 1950s had been spent establishing himself as a cabaret performer in London, the later 1950s were to see the commercial and critical results in a series of enormously profitable appearances in the United States. In the summer of 1955 he appeared at the Desert Inn, Las Vegas (the same year that he had a cameo role in producer Michael Todd's all-star film version of

Noël in his cameo performance in *Around the World in 80 Days* seen here with John Gielgud and Cantinflas

Jules Verne's *Around the World in 80 Days*, in which he played Hesketh-Baggott, the beautifully dressed head of the Employment Agency that finds Passepartout for Phileas Fogg, playing his only scene early in the picture opposite his former understudy John Gielgud). In the autumn he co-starred with Mary Martin in a concert of his own and others' songs *Together With Music* on the American television channel CBS. On the surviving if rather scratchy tape, this is the only opportunity to see Noël sing the songs of Jerome Kern, Rodgers and Hammerstein and others and to regret that he didn't perform them more widely or indeed on record, where virtually all of his many recordings are only of his own words and music.

The success of this, the first-ever live colour concert on American network television led, the following year, to a CBS television production of *Blithe Spirit*, with Noël as Charles Condomine, and then another CBS production of his work in *This Happy Breed*, with Noël as Frank Gibbons, while on Broadway there was a successful revival of *Fallen Angels.*

Back in London his play *South Sea Bubble* was staged at the Lyric, with Vivien Leigh in the role that he had originally written for Gertrude Lawrence with the working title *Island Fling*. *The Times* decided it was 'a minor but not unpleasing Coward' while 'superficial', 'hollow' and 'brittle' were among the other critics' comments. This wasn't vintage Coward, and Miss Leigh was already showing signs of the strain that was to haunt her later life and bring it to an all too early close.

Much more successful was another play, *Nude With Violin*, which had originally and variously been conceived as a vehicle for either Rex Harrison or, more surprisingly, Margaret Rutherford. In the end, it was John Gielgud who played the all-knowing manservant. Gielgud also agreed to direct the play, providing Noël supervise it in a try-out in Dublin, at the Olympia Theatre, before its London debut at the Globe.

Dublin was the choice for the pre-West End try-out because it was now about the only English-speaking city within easy reach of London where Noël would be allowed to spend any time. He had recently chosen to become a tax exile, not – as he made clear – to avoid any payment already due to the Inland Revenue, but rather to circumvent any future demands which he now feared he would be unable to meet at the currently very high rates. His own income was now inevitably less secure as he moved into the last two decades of his life at a time when theatrical and musical fashion was undoubtedly against him – he was, after all, no longer the golden boy of his and his country's Twenties and Thirties.

This decision, one of the very few that Noël was ever to take about his future, came at a time of sudden insecurity about how soon his professional luck might run out, but ironically it caused his career to slump as never before. The concept of tax exile was still very new to the British, who regarded it with deep dislike, seeing it as a lack of patriotism or national pride, especially coming from the man who had written 'The Stately Homes of England', *Cavalcade* and 'London Pride', and so many other plays and songs about what it meant to be English.

So *Nude With Violin* aroused as much controversy over Noël's current tax exile status as it did about its value as a piece of theatre: press headlines at the time accused him of desertion and treachery, and at a time when tax exile is now taken for granted among high earners of all kinds, it is hard to understand or even remember the amount of press hostility which rained down on Coward and by extension all of his work. In that respect, as so often, he took the flak for those who were to follow an easier path abroad.

As a play about the value of modern art – *Nude With Violin* pre-dated Yasmina Reza's hugely popular *Art* by several decades – it was an immediate success in Dublin, but was admired in London only in the context of John Gielgud's performance. Coward took some credit for the latter: *I arrived {in Dublin} to find that Gielgud had directed it with such loving care for my play that he'd forgotten his own performance, so I helped a little with that* – but was castigated for his writing by *The Evening Standard*, which said of it: 'Billed as a comedy, it emerged as a farce and ended as a corpse.'

The play went on to fairly good reviews and business in New York, where it was joined by a revival of *Present Laughter*, and both plays did far better on tour on the West Coast with Noël himself playing the lead-

Noël and John Gielgud standing on O'Connell Bridge in Dublin during the run of *Nude With Violin*

ing roles. Meanwhile in London Gielgud was replaced by Michael Wilding, the film star best known for appearing on screen opposite Anna Neagle. Noël thought he *brought to the play large audiences, immense personal charm and startling inaudibility* and Wilding was followed in his turn by the dancer-director-actor Robert Helpmann, with whom Noël had always maintained a wary friendship, each recognising the threat represented by the polymath other.

The main events of 1956 were directly nothing to do with Noël. On the international political scene there was the Suez crisis (which was, partly, to inspire John Osborne's *The Entertainer*) and, in the theatre, Osborne's revolutionary *Look Back in Anger*.

Noël's response to both events was fairly baleful. Writing in his diary about Suez, he took an uncompromisingly right-wing view of the best way to deal with the Third World: *There is a major crisis over the Suez Canal and a war might occur at any moment, but of course it won't. The idiotic Egyptians are making beasts of themselves and Britain, France and the US are as one in agreeing that the Canal must be international or else. All this could, of course, have been avoided if we had not caved in and been just fair and decent and foolish. We should never have dreamed of evacuating Egypt in the first place. This is obviously a dangerous moment because Russia is supporting Egypt, but my voices tell me that Russia is no more anxious for a full-scale war than we are, so I suppose some compromise will be arrived at. It is the same tedious old story, weak-kneed humanitarianism instead of dignified strength.*

He took an equally dim view of *Look Back in Anger*, the play that was to usher in the age of 'Kitchen Sink' drama and see, almost overnight, the overthrow of previously established theatrical giants like Terence Rattigan and Noël himself. Of course, the style of plays that both men worked within did not, despite a popular misconception to the contrary, become obsolete overnight, and there were many well-crafted and popular 'old-fashioned' plays produced during the 1950s and into the 1960s; but among the literary set who determined the public cultural agenda, Coward, like Rattigan, was seen as belonging firmly to the past.

It was Kenneth Tynan, in an exercise of the power of the theatre critic than modern reviewers can only dream of, who 'made' *Look Back in Anger* when he wrote that he did not feel he could love anyone who didn't like that play.

Noël was aware that Osborne had a talent, referring to his own visit to the Royal Court to see the play as *electrifying . . . Osborne's is a great gift, though I believe it to be composed of vitality rather than anger*, but overall his reaction to the Kitchen Sink school was not unlike Sir Gerald Du Maurier's had been to *The Vortex* – he rubbished it. He was, however, thrown onto the defensive by the new wave of writing, and his comment (about the new hatred of drawing-room drama) that *Duchesses have feelings too!* was that of a man fighting for breath as the surf crashed over him. He was correctly confident in his own talent and knew he still had an audience out there, whatever the theatrical fashion, but he was equally aware, however ruefully, of the fundamental shift that *Look Back in Anger* and its successors represented.

Noël spent 1957 and 1958 touring *Nude With Violin* in the States and keeping out of Britain as much as possible in order to convince the Inland Revenue that he really was domiciled permanently abroad and therefore free of the United Kingdom's then ruinously high tax rates.

The last year of what had proved to be a momentous decade of major flops and growing disenchantment allied to unforeseen successes and (thanks largely to the season in Las Vegas) an enormous income, saw Noël's *Look After Lulu*, a Feydeau adaptation, produced in London and New York, and his appearance in another major film, the Graham Greene/Carol Reed *Our Man in Havana*.

The film, set deep in Greeneland, told of Alec Guinness's vacuum-cleaner salesman accidentally thought to be a spy and treated as such by a wonderfully supercilious Coward as the Man

An unlikely couple, Noël and Ernest Hemingway at Sloppy Joe's, during the filming of *Our Man in Havana*

From MI6 who insists, in the cause of secrecy, in holding his conferences in a Cuban gentlemen's convenience.

Back in England *Look After Lulu* was Noël's adaptation of a Feydeau farce, *Occupy Yourself With Amelia*, which opened at the Royal Court (of all places) in June 1958, in a production starring Vivien Leigh. It had opened a few months earlier in New York, in a production, starring Tammy Grimes, which ran for only 39 performances. The London version also received poor notices but survived them to transfer to the New Theatre later that year. No one now seemed to like Noël's plays except the paying public.

Many of these audiences enjoyed the cinema even more than the theatre, and at this time Noël wrote about the difference between film and stage acting with particular reference to *Our Man in Havana*: *Although the theatre is my first love, I've found certain films fascinating and this was one of them. I had to unlearn all my stage technique; I'm not a very adroit film actor, not technically, and Carol Reed had to stop me overdoing any of my facial expressions. 'Remember', he would say, 'in this shot your lower lip is a foot wide.' I was still playing it all to the back of the gallery.*

He continued to react to bad notices by sailing (or flying) away, and after the first night of *Look After Lulu* in Sloane Square he went on a fortnight's cruise in the Aegean on an Onassis yacht.

In settings like these, and aided by having kept far more of his income than if he were still living in England, he continued through the late 1950s, the 1960s and into his final years, to enjoy a stylish and active social life, mixing with royalty on both sides of the Channel. His long-standing friendship with the Queen Mother didn't prevent him accepting the hospitality of the exiled Duke and Duchess of Windsor in Paris. As an unabashed snob he enjoyed the regal trappings of their lifestyle (there was no sign, in their Paris mansion, of the supposedly democratic and informal approach to life that the public had believed the Duke to hold when he was Prince of Wales), and as a writer he was

A special friendship, Noël and the Queen Mother

fascinated by the private tragedy that the couple were condemned to live out in the long years after the Abdication.

He had always preferred her to him, and this diary entry confirms that this was still the case, a quarter of a century or so after they had first met. She is seen as entertaining, if vain, while the Duke is a pathetic figure: *The Windsor's party was very gay. She is certainly the most charming hostess, and he was extremely amiable. The conversation was mostly general and largely devoted to the question of whether or not the Duchess should have her face lifted. The main consensus was no. Wallis brought this subject up herself with a sort of calculated defiance. I think, however, that she is a curiously honest woman and her sense of humour, particularly about herself, is either profound or brilliantly simulated . . . the Duke and I danced a sailor's hornpipe and the Charleston, but there was no harm in it, perhaps a little sadness and nostalgia for him, and for me a curious feeling of detached amusement, remembering how beastly he had been to and about me in our earlier years when he was Prince of Wales and I was beginning . . .* (Monday 19 January 1959)

Sailing away

The 1960s were to see a late flowering of Coward's talents. Though he was to go into a fairly steep physical decline in the course of the decade (he'd often been in ill health during the 1950s as well), this was to be the decade in which his reputation as a playwright was not only resuscitated but confirmed and celebrated at the National Theatre. He was to write one more hit musical, *Sail Away* (exorcising the memories of *After the Ball*) and one of the most powerful and personal plays of his entire career, *Song at Twilight*.

The decade was also to see him co-starring in films with Laurence Olivier (*Bunny Lake is Missing*) and with Michael Caine (*The Italian Job*) and ended – almost literally – with the seven-day celebration (which he called 'Holy Week') of his 70th birthday in December 1969 across virtually all stage and screen and broadcast media, a multi-faceted celebration which never before or since has been granted to a single entertainer, and one which reflected the sheer diversity and range of his talent to amuse (the title I chose for his and my first biography, published to coincide with the birthday).

The 1960s began, less than auspiciously, with *Waiting in the Wings*, a play set in a retirement home for theatrical veterans (not a million miles away from Denville Hall). This was received with disdain, if not derision, by many critics, who saw it as self-indulgently theatrical and unnecessarily sentimental.

In fact, as so often with Noël's plays, it was much better than it first looked, as has recently been proved by a long-running

1990s Broadway revival with Lauren Bacall and Rosemary Harris. Having been a trustee of Denville Hall for many years, Noël understood perhaps better than anyone the loneliness of the old-age actor of either sex suddenly bereft of relatives, of funding and – worst of all – an audience.

Noël's *Pomp and Circumstance* may have failed to top the best-seller charts but as his first and only novel it has a certain biographical fascination. As in his many short stories, Noël keeps his own character very minimalist and undefined. But the story is based on truth, concerning as it does a sudden and unexpected visit to Jamaica by the then Queen Mother, which caused predictable havoc in the kitchens and drawing rooms of the community, not least at Blue Harbour itself.

One of the joys of being the First Noël is that because he was so versatile and multi-faceted as an actor, dramatist, composer, lyricist, director, novelist and cabaret star, he could always turn from one talent to another. When in these years his plays were not precisely taking London or Broadway by storm, he was still able to make a very healthy living from cabaret, the occasional film

Icons of the old and new showbusiness. Noël with Sean Connery during the filming of *Dr No* in Jamaica. 1961

or television appearance and of course his non-dramatic writing. He also began turning up very discreetly in glossy magazine ads for his beloved Jamaica.

Accordingly, he spent 1961 – a year otherwise distinguished

only by his appearance in an NBC television production of *Brief Encounter*, where he played the Trevor Howard role of Alec Harvey – writing *Sail Away*, which he directed himself when it opened that year in New York.

Given the way the critics seemed to be gunning for him in London, it's entirely understandable that he should have chosen a Broadway opening. The subject matter – a romance on a cruise ship – and the star, Elaine Stritch, also made a New York opening eminently sensible, and the show, which has some wonderful numbers, was a well-deserved hit. This was indeed where Stritch became a Broadway star, Noël having recognised her potential on the pre-opening tour.

Sail Away opened in Boston at the Colonial Theatre, with a first night audience that included Jackie Kennedy, and on Broadway in October, where this story of a shipboard romance was sufficiently well received for Noël to transfer it to London in late June the following year, after a try-out at Bristol.

The title song was in fact one that Noël had written several years earlier as a cabaret number, but as a show, *Sail Away* now became the last Broadway and West End musical for which he wrote both words and music. The plot was – to say the least – fragile, but it did make a star of Elaine Stritch, who started rehearsals with a relatively minor role and was only promoted over the title and given virtually all the best songs when it was reckoned that the original leading lady, Jean Fenn, although excellent, was rather too operatic for a musical comedy:

When the storm clouds are riding through a winter sky
Sail away – sail away
When the love-light is fading in your sweetheart's eye
Sail away – sail away.
When you feel your song is orchestrated wrong
Why should you prolong

Your stay?
When the wind and the weather blow your dreams sky high
Sail away – sail away – sail away!

The song itself, and the show from which it came, were peculiarly autobiographical, not that Noël had any real time for package tourism or cruise liners in particular, but because the idea of sailing away whenever storm clouds were riding had been absolutely central to his life.

From the moment that his fortunes allowed, he would regularly set sail for sunnier climes than Britain – not only to escape a flop or any kind of career setback, but also to move on even from a hit, convinced that a change of scenery would spur him on to the next project. Like Somerset Maugham, he also believed that characters met in transit would provide superb copy for his short stories, and indeed many of these are specifically set in locations he had visited by ship.

His love of the sea had also led to a life-long passion for the Royal Navy, for which he had already been asked by his friend Louis Mountbatten to select the recreational movies, and where again he found in mess and officer's wardrooms alike the kind of segregated, separated society he had always most envied and enjoyed.

His passions for male company, for the stiff upper lip, for grace under pressure and for any escape from what he now found to be the stifling normality of shore life were all satisfied at sea, where he became an observant passenger rather than the focus of all attention.

And then of course there were the destinations. He had always found in the Far East the kind of sunshine he craved, but now he began to find, in Hawaii and Bermuda and ultimately Jamaica, not only the sun but the sea and sand and sexual freedom that he also craved and found so absent from Little Britain.

Sail Away also included two other wonderful numbers, the first an exasperated, comic question that most travellers have asked ever since, each of them unaware that the same may be being asked of them by their fellow cruise-ship (or airplane, or tourist resort) passengers:

> *Why do the wrong people travel, travel, travel,*
> *When the right people stay back home?*
> *What peculiar obsessions*
> *Inspire those processions*
> *Of families from Houston, Tex,*
> *With all those cameras round their necks?*
> *They will take a train*
> *Or an aeroplane*
> *For an hour on the Costa Brava,*
> *And they'll see Pompeii*
> *On the only day*
> *That it's up to its ass in molten lava.*
> *It would take years to unravel – ravel – ravel*
> *Every impulse that makes them roam*
> *But why oh why do the wrong people travel*
> *When the right people stay back home*
> *With all that Kleenex,*
> *When the right people stay back home*
> *With all that lettuce*
> *When the right people stay back home*
> *With all those Kennedys?*
> *Won't someone tell me*
> *Why the right*
> *I say the right people stay back home?*

Another slyly satirical song written by Noël at this time both satirised the elderly ladies whom Coward had seen disembarking on Capri (*Every single one of them* determined *to have themselves a ball!*) and celebrated the liberating effects of sunshine and an easy sexuality. This latter was something he had also touched on in *Brief Encounter*, where Laura (Celia Johnson) wonders whether warmer weather wouldn't bring the English out of their sexless, shy shell:

> *In a bar on the Piccolo Marina*
> *Life called to Mrs Wentworth-Brewster,*
> *Fate beckoned and introduced her*
> *Into a rather queer*
> *Unfamiliar atmosphere.*
> *She'd just sit there, propping up the bar*
> *Beside a fisherman who sang to a guitar.*
> *When accused of having gone too far*
> *She merely cried, 'Funiculi!*
> *Just fancy me!*
> *Funicula!'*
> *When he bellowed 'Che Bella Signora!'*
> *Sheer ecstasy at once produced a*
> *Wild shriek from Mrs Wentworth-Brewster,*
> *Changing her whole demeanour.*
> *When both her daughters and her son said,*
> *'Please come home, Mama,'*
> *She murmured rather bibulously, 'Who d'you think you are?'*
> *Nobody can afford to be so lahdy-bloody-da*
> *In a bar on the Piccolo Marina . . .*
>
> *Her family, in floods of tears, cried,*
> *'Leave these men, Mama.'*
> *She said, 'They're just high-spirited, like all Italians are*
> *And most of them have a great deal more to offer than*
> *Papa*
> *In a bar on the Piccolo Marina.'*

Sail Away brought Stritch to London – and to the Savoy, Noël's favourite hotel, where she was, on future occasions, to virtually take up residence when in London. Having triumphantly brought the show and its star to the West End, Noël returned to the States in 1963. He was, in these last 10 years of his life, to have two more musicals on Broadway, though neither was entirely his own work. The first was *The Girl Who Came to Supper*, a musical version of Terence Rattigan's *The Sleeping Prince*, which Olivier had already filmed with Marilyn Monroe as *The Prince and the Showgirl*. The plot concerned the Coronation of George V and a chorus girl who comes to spend the night with a visiting Ruritanian Prince.

Neither Jose Ferrer nor Florence Henderson had quite the required charisma however, and although Noël's score was both brilliant and enchanting (including as it did an entire sequence of 'turn of the century' London pub songs which Tessie O'Shea sang in the one true moment of genius that the whole evening

Travel was his preferred therapy.
Noël steps off the *Queen Mary*

provided), it was not a success, nor has it ever been seen in London, despite the fact that its producers coming off the back of *My Fair Lady* thought it might prove a suitable successor.

Two years later, there was to be one more part-Coward musical on Broadway and in the West End: this was *High Spirits*, based on Noël's *Blithe Spirit* on which Hugh Martin and Timothy Gray had long been working. Although he had taken his time in giving it the green light, Noël, as was still his wont, came in to rehearsals as a kind of advisor/script doctor and, at the request of the original star, Tammy Grimes, even wrote some of the lyrics, the very last of his new ones ever to be heard on a stage.

At this time, as if to confirm his versatility, he also published a third collection of short stories, and introduced on Granada Television a sequence of four of his plays (*Present Laughter*, *Blithe Spirit*, *The Vortex* and *Design for Living*).

In many ways the best thing about *The Girl Who Came to Supper* is Noël's brilliant evocation of the world of the Edwardian operetta and music hall, especially in Tessie O'Shea's 'Saturday Night at the Rose and Crown':

> *Saturday night at the Rose and Crown,*
> *That's just the place to be,*
> *Tinkers and Tailors*
> *And Soldiers and Sailors*
> *All out for a bit of a spree,*
> *If you find that you're*
> *Weary of life*
> *With your trouble and strife*
> *And the kids have got you down*
> *It will all come right*
> *On Saturday night*
> *At the Rose and Crown.*

Singing at twilight

The major of event of 1964 was Laurence Olivier's decision to revive *Hay Fever* for the National Theatre, in a year which also saw a quartet of Coward plays on British television and the gradual, grudging realisation that the old Master was not only still alive, but still more prolific and versatile than many entertainers only a third of his age. But gratifying though it was to be taken seriously by British television as well as by its American counterpart, it was the National Theatre's *Hay Fever* that was crucial to Noël's renaissance as perhaps the greatest living British theatrical icon, in sharp contrast to the elderly tax exile, which had become the fate of many of his surviving contemporaries.

Hay Fever was chosen by Olivier, over *Private Lives* and *Design for Living*, as it offered the chance for company playing rather than just vehicles for stars, though naturally enough he cast one as Judith Bliss – Dame Edith Evans. True, she was too old for the role (by about 20 years), and had trouble remembering her lines. She was supposed to say, in the course of the play, 'On a clear day you can see Marlow' but insisted on saying, despite being corrected many times by Noël, 'On a very clear day you can see Marlow'. Eventually he snapped, *No, Edith, on a* very *clear day you can see Marlowe and Beaumont and Fletcher!*

'So you have been nationalised at last!' Terence Rattigan exclaimed somewhat enviously to Noël, early in 1964, when Olivier, Kenneth Tynan and the director John Dexter got together to offer him this production of *Hay Fever*, one which starred not only Dame Edith, but Maggie Smith, Lynn Redgrave, Derek

Jacobi and Robert Lang, a cast, as Noël noted, who could have played a telephone directory out loud, let alone a vintage comedy which had always run like clockwork. For Maggie Smith especially, this was an introduction to the gangling, high-camp brand of comedy which she was to epitomise in a later *Private Lives*.

If *Hay Fever* was the main event of 1964, then an interesting minor one was *High Spirits*, the musical version of *Blithe Spirit*. This had a score by Hugh Martin and Timothy Gray, and starred Edward Woodward as Charles, with Tammy Grimes as Elvira and Bea Lillie as Madame Arcati, and Noël directed it himself, adding only a few lines (in the number 'Home Sweet Heaven') to the script. It was first staged for Broadway, with Cicely Coutneidge heading the later London cast.

In 1965 Noël appeared on film again, playing a landlord in the thriller *Bunny Lake is Missing*. This was a seedy, lecherous old landlord, not at all the public image of the suave playboy that had sustained him for decades, and he enjoyed acting against type. He was also pleased to be in a film with Laurence Olivier, and other stars in the cast included Martita Hunt and Anna Massey – along with the American actor Keir Dullea. I was with Noël at his regular suite in the Savoy, talking to him about the biography that I was writing, when Dullea knocked on the door. *Come in!* said Noël. 'Ah, Mr Coward . . . I'm appearing with you in *Bunny Lake is Missing*, and I thought I'd introduce myself here before we meet on set . . . I'm Keir Dullea.' *Keir Dullea,* Noël shot back, *Gone Tomorrow!*

Noël's health declined in 1966, with his short-term memory, especially for lines, noticeably fading. Despite this, he was determined to appear in the trio of plays – *Song at Twilight*, *Shadows of the Evening* and *Come Into the Garden, Maud* – that were presented in London under the title *Suite in Three Keys*, though his poor health delayed rehearsals and made him unable to take the plays as planned on to Broadway. Of these plays, the latter two were one-act

The man in the mirror. Noël reflected in his study at Les Avants in Switzerland

comedies and dramas of only routine interest, but *Song at Twilight* retains considerable autobiographical fascination as the only drama he ever wrote about homosexuality and the closeted life. Despite his diaries (which I co-edited with Graham Payn), and his two completed autobiographies, Noël's remains one of the great conjuring tricks of the 20th century. Now you see him, now you don't.

'Such a cunning little mystery, all done with mirrors' says Elyot to Amanda about death at the end of *Private Lives*, and that was not the only mystery. How this suburban boy from South London became the playboy of the West End world is still only really explained by the sheer level of his own ambition, energy and expertise.

But what of his private life? We know that he was gay for half a century; we know there were long relationships with Louis Hayward, Jack Wilson, Alan Webb and Graham Payn, who became his lifelong partner, friend and executor, the man who still keeps the Coward flag flying.

There were also, of course, many briefer encounters with actors, singers and dancers, but because these were exclusively male and in a safely closed world behind the stage door, Noël was obliged by the fashion and indeed the criminal laws of the time to keep his homosexuality a well-buried secret. True, he was 'out' to a large number of friends, colleagues and acquaintances, whom he would even entertain with a gay re-write of his legendary torch song, 'Mad About the Boy'. But nowhere in his writing, not even in his diaries, does he begin to explore his own homosexuality – all you find there is a burst of outrage when John Gielgud is arrested for soliciting: *Poor, silly, idiotic, foolish, careless John . . . how could he, how could he, have been so stupid and so selfish?*

Noël did not get his own knighthood until 1970, almost 20 years after John had been arrested only days after his own, and he always believed that the Gielgud arrest heightened an already anti-gay feeling within the Establishment.

So is there nowhere to turn if we are to search for Noël's own view? Well, yes there is, although I didn't find it until long after he died. Noël's last work for the London stage was this 1966 *Suite in Three Keys* trilogy, in which he made his last stage appearances as one of three players, the others being Lilli Palmer and Irene Worth. Two of the three dark comedies made up a double bill and are immensely forgettable; but the third play, and by far the most important, is *Song at Twilight*, which in 1998, I was lucky enough to be invited to direct, first at the King's Head Theatre in Islington and then for a year in the West End, with Corin and Vanessa Redgrave and Kika Markham.

Noël himself, who was writing these plays at the time I was first writing his life, always said that *Song* is really based on either Somerset Maugham or Max Beerbohm in retirement, but I am much more inclined to believe that it is the most directly and painfully autobiographical of all Coward's 40-plus plays. It concerns a veteran and hugely distinguished Nobel prize-winning novelist living out his old age in what is clearly a marriage of convenience to his former secretary. They have taken up residence, not unlike Vladimir Nabokov, in a Swiss hotel, where they are visited by a wonderfully bitchy former movie star who is now writing her memoirs and wants the author to sign his notable name to her preface.

The author refuses, and in revenge the star threatens to 'out' him, whereupon he reacts so violently that she asks him what on earth, in this day and age, he finds so frightening about telling his readers the truth of his sex life. The author, Sir Hugo Latymer, replies in a speech through which, I believe, you can hear the voice of Noël Coward more loudly and more clearly than in anything else either musical or dramatic that he ever wrote:

Even when the actual law ceases to exist, there will still be a stigma attached to 'the love that dare not speak its name' in the minds of millions of people for generations to come. It takes more than a few outspoken books and plays and clever speeches in Parliament to uproot moral prejudice from the Anglo-Saxon mind. And that, in less than a hundred words, is a precise summary of Noël's attitude towards his own sexuality. The subsequent fashion for 'coming out' would have struck him as nothing more than self-indulgent exhibitionism and, as with another British actor long exiled abroad (Sir Dirk Bogarde), there was also a very strong and realistic feeling that any revelation of the truth would do nothing but harm at his box office.

But Noël found the run of *Suite in Three Keys* physically exhausting, especially at the weekends, when they would perform all three plays across matinees and evenings. It had been 10 years since he had last appeared on stage in the American tour of *Nude With Violin* and *Present Laughter*, and frighteningly his memory was now very shaky indeed. He was also suffering from various relatively minor medical complications and therefore increasingly inclined to retire to his two beloved homes, the one nestling under the Swiss Alps at Les Avants, and the other out in the mid-day sun of Blue Harbour in Jamaica.

Out in the midday sun: Jamaica

It was just after the Second World War that Noël had fallen in love not with a person but a place, and that place was of course Jamaica. For a South London boy, born in Teddington and brought up in Battersea in almost constantly bad weather, the idea of a place in the sun had become especially seductive, especially considering that in early life, if he did ever get to the seaside, it was usually the rain-swept pebbles of Brighton or Bognor Regis.

His discovery of Jamaica in the late 1940s was something else entirely. He had fallen for the island while staying at a house called Goldeneye, where Ian Fleming wrote the first of his James Bond books, and which Noël, a somewhat uneasy tenant, rapidly rechristened Golden Eye, Nose and Throat because of the rising damp. He also took a dim view of Ivor Novello's beach-front home on the same island.

But he had of course long been an inveterate and inexhaustible traveller: *I am always, I find, arriving just too late; I get to Japan just after the Cherry Blossom has fallen, I reach New England just after the Foliage Season. People abroad are always telling me of something I have just missed. I find this very restful.*

Noël in such diverse works as *South Sea Bubble* and *Pacific 1860* had always fantasised an island called Samolo, but the reality was Jamaica, where he found true late-life happiness as a painter, as a swimmer, as a writer and as a host.

Jamaica after the war offered peace, warmth, and a kind of freedom from the increasingly restrictive climate, both artistically and sexually, of Europe and America. Jamaica was always open, never chilly, and it allowed him vistas to paint in the one late-life career he found truly satisfying, although (as he never sold a painting in his lifetime) totally unprofitable.

Noël had in fact begun painting as a child – at the age of 10 he signed what he called 'Nell Gwynne', in fact a garish study looking more like the Scarecrow from the *Wizard of Oz*. Then, throughout the 1930s, on the rare weekends at Goldenhurst in Kent, when he wasn't either in rehearsal or working on a new score, he went back to the easel and one Sunday drove over to Chartwell, to visit Winston Churchill, with whom he maintained a long if occasionally rather edgy friendship.

Winston commanded him to stop painting in watercolours and to work only in oils, and gradually these became the most favourite and time-consuming of all his non-theatrical pastimes. The countless hours he spent at his easel were among the most happy and carefree of his entire life. But Noël himself was as always the sharpest critic of his own work. Writing in his 1955 diary he noted: *My paintings have a sense of colour and design and do at least convey a fantasised impression of Jamaica but as yet I am still at a stage where I break rules without really having learned them.*

He could be equally critical of others when it came to painting: *All you ever think of* he once said to his art-struck secretary Cole Lesley, *is 'Monet, Monet, Monet'*, but his own work gave pleasure to his friends as well as to himself (despite his awareness of his own limitations), and in

His favourite hobby. Noël and one of his paintings at a charity auction

return for my book about him he once gave me a wonderfully evocative little beach scene inscribed on the back *From my touch and Gaugin period*, which I still cherish. In truth, Noël could never quite manage figures, which is why his beach scenes are always peopled by tiny matchstick men; he also painted Jamaica not precisely as he saw it, from his Blue Harbour balcony, but as it would have looked on the countless backdrops in front of which he had spent his life as an actor.

Like those of Oliver Messel and Cecil Beaton, his great designer contemporaries in the West End and on Broadway, Noël's paintings of Jamaica are undoubtedly theatrical, but they are warmed by an unmistakeable love of the land and seascape. It is no accident that the only commercials that he ever wrote were for the Jamaica tourist board.

First at Blue Harbour, which remained his holiday home for the last quarter-century of his life, and then at Firefly, the bare little retreat he built above it in which to write and read (and where he was to die). Noël really found late-life happiness with his companions Graham Payn and Cole Lesley, who had been with him since before the war and really were now his family.

Although he enjoyed entertaining at Blue Harbour, by this stage of his life visitors were limited to the oldest of friends, always of course including Marlene Dietrich, who once complained that their other friends seemed hardly to be lasting at all. 'I count myself lucky', she said, 'if indeed they last through lunch.'

The following year, 1967, he appeared in Richard Rodgers' television musical *Androcles and the Lion*, playing Caesar and also published the aptly-named *Bon Voyage*, a third collection of his short stories.

In 1968 he appeared as The Witch of Capri in Tennessee Williams's film *Boom*, based on Williams's play *The Milk Train Doesn't Stop Here Any More*. This was a Gothic venture, also starring Elizabeth Taylor and Richard Burton at the height of their fame, and directed by Jo Losey. It was also the first of three last films (the others being *Bunny Lake is Missing* and the original *Italian Job*), for all of which Coward was cast against type, and at last allowed to escape from the smooth, svelte, impeccably clenched image conveyed by virtually all his earlier films.

Camp doesn't come much higher than *Boom*: of Noël, as the sinister stranger, it was said, as with every one of his screen appearances over the last 15 years, that he had stolen the picture. The trouble was, as he noted, that it amounted here to petty larceny.

Meanwhile, he was being represented on stage by *Noël Coward's Sweet Potato*, the first of three late revues (the others being *Oh Coward!* and *Cowardy Custard*) which were to celebrate just a few of the 400 songs he had by now written.

The decade ended on a high, with Noël's 70th birthday. This was preceded by his *Italian Job* appearance as a deeply royalist

From enfant terrible to national treasure: a late portrait of Noël

criminal whose prison cell was like a pared-down version of his suite at the Savoy, while *Private Lives* was revived at the Billy Rose Theatre in New York with Maggie Smith and John Standing replacing an ailing Robert Stephens.

At around this time, when a reporter in Melbourne had asked 'What is your idea of an ideal private life?' he had replied simply *Mine.* And everything came together at the 70th, when Noël finally ceased being an *enfant terrible* or a middle-aged satirist and became quite simply the grand old man of theatre, commanding respect for his long list of achievements and being accorded an almost awed reverence for his sheer, triumphant survival.

There was, within what he called Holy Week, a celebration of his movies at the National Film Theatre, of his plays and songs on BBC radio and television, an all-star stage gala at the Phoenix Theatre (based on his and my first biography, and also called *A Talent to Amuse*) and a banquet at the Savoy Hotel for which the speakers included Laurence Olivier and Lord Mountbatten, just two of the many Establishment figures who had been with Noël almost since the very beginning.

The after-dinner speeches were televised, and you can still feel the frisson of nervous embarrassment that ran through the room when Noël, having risen to his feet, said *I have had two great loves in my life . . .*

Homosexuality was now legal, but this was not, in front of the television cameras, and in such distinguished company, the place to come out of the closet, surely? The next sentence visibly released the tension: *One has been the Theatre and the other the Sea . . .* and he then paid compliments to the two representatives of those loves – Olivier for the theatre, Mountbatten for the sea.

There was only one way to top this celebration of a career that had more or less spanned the century, and that was by the long-awaited and grotesquely overdue knighthood, which finally arrived in 1970. It had not been Noël's homosexuality as much as his many years of tax exile that had delayed the honour. A man who, despite appearing on stage in London from time to time, or in British films, chose to divide his life between Switzerland, Jamaica and the United States (principally New York) and who was clearly at odds with the politics and social trends of modern British life, was hardly the highest candidate for a knighthood, especially from Harold Wilson's Labour government. MBEs for the Beatles to court the youth vote were far more Wilson's style – the man in the Gannex raincoat and pipe had very little sympathy for the man with a silk dressing gown and cigarette holder.

Noël did, however, have friends at Court – not least the Queen, the Queen Mother and Princess Margaret, and not forgetting the Windsors' would-be *éminence grise*, Lord Louis Mountbatten. So it was that, flanked by two of his oldest theatrical female friends – the designer Gladys Calthrop and the actress Joyce Carey – Noël finally (and, to be fair, with the Prime Minister's acceptance) received the tap on the shoulder from the Queen and emerged from the Palace into a blaze of flashbulbs as Sir Noël Coward.

Noël at Buckingham Palace after his Knighthood. 1970

This might, had his health been better, have been an inducement to write another play, as he would have loved to have shown not only that he could still hack it and that plays set among the upper middle classes were still commercially successful, but that a theatre knight could hold his own against younger, scruffier, more 'socially aware' competitors.

That this was not to be was evident to his friends, who were saddened at the obvious and increasingly rapid decline in his health that led, in effect, to his complete retirement for the last few years of his life. He was pleased that two revues based on his work, *Oh, Coward!* in New York and *Cowardy Custard* in London, both took place in 1972, just as he had been by the further revival of *Hay Fever* in New York, at the Helen Hayes Theatre in 1970 – where, however, it only managed a couple of dozen performances.

He made the occasional, gallant, public appearance, by now holding firmly the arm of his companion (Dietrich as often as not, or Merle Oberon), but chose mainly to spend time with his closest circle of friends. He no longer had the physical energy for writing, let alone acting, and, in the words of one of his songs, there comes a time when everyone should call it a day and leave the stage to a new generation:

Why must the show go on?
It can't be all that indispensable,
To me it really isn't sensible
On the whole
To play a leading role
While fighting those tears you can't control,
Why kick up your legs
When draining the dregs
Of sorrow's bitter cup?
Because you have read
Some idiot has said,
'The curtain must go up'!
I'd like to know why a star takes bows
Having just returned from burying her spouse.
Brave boop-a-doopers,
Go home and dry your tears,
Gallant old troupers,
You've bored us all for years
And when you're so blue,
Wet through
And thoroughly woe-begone,
Why must the show go on?
Oh Mammy!
Why must the show go on?

It was while he was spending the winter as usual in his beloved Jamaica, that he died, on the night of the 25 March 1973: he was just over 73 years old.

Noël's last evening was spent with his long-time partner, Graham Payn, and his long-serving valet and then secretary and close friend Cole Lesley – known to everyone as 'Coley'. Writing in his own memoir, *My Life With Noël Coward*, Graham Payn recalled: 'His last evening was like any other, with drinks and chat and lots of laughs with him up at Firefly until, like Mrs Wentworth-Brewster [the heroine of his song "A Bar on the Piccolo

Noël relaxing at Firefly, his Jamaican retreat, with Graham Payn and Joyce Carey

Marina"], Coley and I would "totter down the hill". Noël had always enjoyed privacy but lately it had become a necessity which Coley and I respected. As we took our leave that evening, Noël called out "Goodnight, my darlings. See you in the morning!" We left him sitting in his chair on the terrace, his wire-rimmed glasses perched on the end of his nose, and a copy of E S Nesbit's *The Enchanted Castle* propped up in front of him, with *The Would-Be-Goods* close by.

'Early next morning Imogen, Miguel's wife [Miguel was the housekeeper/handyman at Firefly] came rushing down to Blue Harbour to inform us breathlessly that "Master" was not well. We immediately rang for the doctor and raced up the hill.

'What happened is perhaps most vividly recounted by Miguel, who ran the house for us: "My wife, Imogen, passing by around six a.m. and she hear moaning from the bathroom. It was unusual, since Master like to sleep in. She came get me. First I don't want to go 'cause he get very mad if he disturbed, but she say, 'Something wrong there'. I go to the door and say, 'Master, Master, let me in. It's me, Miguel, but he don't answer so I get a ladder and climb to the window. I hear more moaning so I break the shutter and see Master lying on the bathroom floor. I tell my wife, 'Go quick to Blue Harbour and fetch Mr. Payn and Mr. Lesley.' I pick Master up and take him to the bed. He was rubbing at his chest. He open his eyes and say, 'Miguel, where's Mr. Payn and Mr. Lesley?' I say, 'They coming, sir', then he reach up and pat me twice on the shoulder and say, 'Never mind, Miguel, never mind.' I know he's gone. His teeth came out, so I put them back, then I came to the balcony. The car arrive with Mr. Payn and Mr. Lesley. Mr. Lesley jump out but I call and say 'Master gone, sir.' Mr. Lesley say, 'Stop it, Miguel. Don't say that.' I say, 'It's true, sir; Master gone, sir.' Mr Lesley put his hands on top of his head and he go spinning around on the lawn with tears streaming down.'''

Noël had never been afraid of death, or of what lay after – he was convinced that there was nothing – but he regretted that he wouldn't be around for the party any more, as in this diary entry from the 1950s indicates:

It sickens me that a world so potentially exciting and enjoyable should be so beset by dark fears and superstitious mysticism. There is so much that is, and will always be, unexplained. Why not get on with the material and experience at hand and try to make the best of it? . . . Death seems to me as natural a process as birth; inevitable, absolute and final. If, when it happens to me, I find myself in a sort of Odeon ante-room queuing up for an interview with Our Lord, I shall be very surprised indeed . . . the only thing that really saddens me over my demise is that I shall not be here to read the nonsense that will be written about me and my works and my motives. There will be books proving conclusively that I was a homosexual and books proving equally conclusively that I was not. There will be detailed and inaccurate analyses of my writing this or that and of my character. There will be lists of apocryphal jokes I never made and gleeful misquotations of words I never said. What a pity I shan't be here to enjoy them! (Saturday 19 March 1955)

Equally to the point, and more pithily expressed, was this relatively brief poem:

> *I'm here for a short visit only*
> *And I'd rather be loved than hated*
> *Eternity may be lonely*
> *When my body's disintegrated*
> *And that which is loosely termed my soul*
> *Goes whizzing off through the infinite*
> *By means of some remote control*
> *I'd like to think I was missed a bit.*

Naturally he was. He still is.

Epilogue

There were two Coward shows playing at the time of Noël's death, neither of them plays, but musical anthologies of some of his 400 or so songs. In New York, *Oh, Coward!* was a three-handed intimate revue at which he had made his last public appearance, suitably escorted by Marlene Dietrich, while in London the lights were lowered all along Shaftesbury Avenue when he died and most notably of course outside *Cowardy Custard* – another anthology of his musical work but this one with an all-British cast led by Patricia Routledge and John Moffat.

Another Coward revue was requested, early in the 1980s, by the Hong Kong Festival and as they had already had *Cowardy Custard* and *Oh, Coward!* they required something rather different. At that time, following a request Noël had made to me not long before his death, I had written the first full biography of Gertrude Lawrence and using this as well as my life of Noël, I put together an early version of my *Noël and Gertie*, which starred two actors (Gary Bond and Maria Aitken) and two singers (Mark Winter and Liz Robertson). This ran not only for a week in Hong Kong but also at the King's Head in Islington, where Simon Cadell and Joanna Lumley inherited the leading roles.

I was still narrating the show myself, but had realised that having five of us (two actors, two singers and one host) was getting a little crowded for a small stage and a show with only two in its title. Accordingly I took the script and converted it into a two-hander, which duly opened at the Donmar in July 1985 with Lewis Fiander and Patricia Hodge – William Blezard at the piano.

A year later, it opened at the Comedy in a production by Alan Strachan with Simon Cadell and again Patricia Hodge, with Jonathan Cohen at the piano. Over all this time, the show has proved surprisingly durable: it ran almost a year at the Comedy and has since then been in production all over the world. And *Noël and Gertie* entered the 21st century under its American title *If Love Were All*, in a production by Leigh Lawson starring Twiggy and Harry Groener, that ran for nine months off Broadway at the theatre named after Lucille Lortel. When it first opened in London, the late critic Milton Shulman was kind enough to say in the *Evening Standard* that it should keep the box office busy for many months, and happily for us all it has done just that world-wide for two entire decades.

In terms of his dramas and comedies, Noël now ranks among the highest of all those playwrights produced by local British amateur dramatic societies, with *Blithe Spirit* heading the list of more than 30 revivals a year and this has also been the comedy most often revived in the West End – most recently at the Savoy with Penelope Keith breaking the mould of Margaret Rutherford as an unusual Madame Arcati.

Private Lives has also frequently been revived, though Noël's own warning to actors that it was a lot harder to play than it looked proved painfully true when Elizabeth Taylor and Richard Burton took on the leading roles in a catastrophic Broadway revival in 1983.

London revivals of that play have been much more successful. There have been at least half a dozen since Maggie Smith and Robert Stephens (another real-life marriage in trouble) played it in the West End in 1973, with Stephens replaced on a long tour and then on Broadway by John Standing. Since then there has been one National Theatre revival and several in the West End, including one starring Maria Aitken and Michael Jayston; the most recent was one starring Alan Rickman and Lindsay Duncan, which ran at the Albery before transferring for an equally successful season in New York.

The Albery was also the home of a very strong production of *Hay Fever*, with Maria Aitken as Judith Bliss. Aitken became something of a Coward specialist, for which the requirements are an ineffably vague elegance, a long neck and that sense (especially valuable for Elvira) of having drifted in from some other planet.

One of Aitken's other major Coward roles, round the corner at the Garrick, was as Florence Lancaster in a rare revival of Noël's first success, *The Vortex*, which came from Philip Prowse at the Glasgow Citizens'. Prowse has been, for many years now, one of the most innovative and dedicated of Coward directors, with an extraordinarily brave *Cavalcade* for the turn of the last century. Given that this normally requires a cast of over 100, to start both it and the equally massive *Semi-Monde* on the stage of the Glasgow Citizens showed, in financially embattled times, a willingness to tackle the most challenging and difficult of Coward rather than the easy route of the small-cast light comedies chosen by so many others.

The Vortex was also the play chosen by Michael Grandage to open his first season as Artistic Director of the Donmar, with Chiwetel Ejiofor and Francesca Annis, and a memorable performance by Bette Bourne as Pawnie.

One indication that Coward's reputation remains equally high on both sides of the Atlantic was the commissioning and unveiling of three identical statues. One by his grave in his beloved Jamaica, and one each in the foyers of the Theatre Royal, Drury Lane and the Gershwin Theatre on Broadway. At the front of each of these, flowers are laid on 16 December, Noël's birthday, by a star who has been associated with his work. To no other entertainer is this annual tribute paid.

He also has, perhaps the greatest honour of all, a plaque in Westminster Abbey unveiled by his life-long friend, Her Majesty

Queen Elizabeth the Queen Mother, and to my huge private delight, bearing the words 'A Talent to Amuse', although the quotation is of course his own (from the song 'If Love Were All').

Among many celebrations here and abroad, for Noël's centenary, I put together an all-star BBC Radio 2 concert which included Edward Fox reading one of the long-lost wartime poems, 'Lie in the Dark and Listen'; in the same broadcast, Simon Williams and Lucy Fleming played a scene from her mother Celia Johnson's *Brief Encounter,* while the late Hubert Gregg, writer and singer of one great London wartime song ('Maybe It's Because I'm a Londoner') sang the other, Noël's 'London Pride'.

Around this time it was also decided by Noël's executors (among them Graham Payn and Dany Dasto) that Noël's papers, scripts, manuscripts and scores should be left somewhere for easy access by both students of his work and those directors, actors and designers who were involved in reviving them.

Under its Head of Drama, the playwright David Edgar, space was dedicated for a Noël Coward Study Centre in the library of Birmingham University, and since then many bequests, not least by Graham Payn himself, have ensured that this remains the definitive archive for all those interested in any kind of Coward research. Again, outside of Shakespeare and Wilde and Arthur Miller, it is hard to think of another playwright accorded such everlasting attention.

Added to this, there has been the foundation – both here and in New York – of a Noël Coward Society, largely made up of theatregoers who wish to celebrate his memory. They organise the flower-laying at the feet of the statues, and also publish a monthly magazine with details of forthcoming productions and reviews of those already up and running.

What is the most enduring legacy that Coward has left us? Is it his comedy? His music? Is it his sense of style, or of Britishness, the latter of all the stronger an appeal for coming at a time when the class system has crashed, the Royal Navy been reduced to a fraction of its former self and the Empire become, as Rudyard Kipling predicted 'As one with Nineveh and Tyre'?

I suppose, ultimately, it is all of these, together with a fascination felt for a man who not only epitomised an era but very largely helped to create it – in the public mind, at least. He would have appreciated the irony that even where he sought to make fun of it, as in 'Mad Dogs and Englishmen', the public took it as a compliment.

If ever the dictum 'The secret of success is hard work' was proved through one man's career, it is through Coward's. His sheer energy, allied to an extraordinary talent – or talents, rather, given his abilities as playwright, composer, lyricist, director, actor and poet – were astonishing. And although the strain surfaced every now and then in the form of nervous collapses – not to mention a history of stress-related illnesses and a relatively early death – this energy gave expression to these talents, and earned him the richly deserved title of Master. This was a title awarded decades before the State belatedly gave him an honour, and, for all the pleasure that the knighthood brought, it was one that better symbolised the respect in which he was held by the theatre world.

A man who liked to have his life well-ordered and comfortable, and to be firmly at the centre of long-lasting relationships, he found the temporary 'madness' of falling in love a subversive, difficult and occasionally excruciating experience. He recorded this remarkably frankly in his poem, 'I Am No Good at Love':

> I am no good at love
> My heart should be wise and free
> I kill the unfortunate golden goose
> Whoever it may be
> With over-articulate tenderness
> And too much intensity

I am no good at love
I batter it out of shape
Suspicion tears at my sleepless mind
And, gibbering like an ape,
I lie alone in the endless dark
Knowing there's no escape

I am no good at love
When my easy heart I yield
Wild words come tumbling from my mouth
Which should have stayed concealed;
And my jealousy turns a bed of bliss
Into a battlefield.

I am no good at love
I betray it with little sins
For I feel the misery of the end
In the moment that it begins
And the bitterness of the last good-bye
Is the bitterness that wins.

His poetry, which is often elegiac, is still known primarily to Coward addicts, the general public remaining aware only of his songs and plays. His last poem, the one we found unfinished by his bedside in Jamaica when he died there, has a haunting, elegiac quality and as it ended his life as a writer and a man, so it should end this brief study of his life and work:

When I have fears, as Keats had fears,
Of the moment I'll cease to be
I console myself with vanished years
Remember laughter, remembered tears,
And the peace of the changing sea.

When I feel sad, as Keats felt sad,
That my life is so nearly done
It gives me comfort to dwell upon
Remembered friends who are dead and gone
And the jokes we had and the fun.

How happy they are I cannot know
But happy am I who loved them so.

Horst Tappe's complimentary late portrait of Noël at home in Switzerland

Chronology

Year	Age	Life
1899		Born on 16 December in Teddington, Middlesex.
1911	12	Made first stage appearance in *The Goldfish*, London.
1914	15	Began writing songs, sketches and short stories (with Esme Wynne).
1917	18	His play, *Ida Collaborates* (written with Esme Wynne) produced on a British tour.
1918	19	Wrote his first play as sole author, *The Rat Trap*, produced in Britain in 1926.
1919	20	Wrote *I'll Leave it to You*, produced in Britain in 1920 and in USA in 1923.
1921	22	Wrote *The Young Idea*, produced in Britain in 1922 and in USA in 1923.
1922	23	Wrote songs and sketches for the revue *London Calling!* produced in 1923, and *The Queen Was in the Parlour*, produced in Britain in 1926 and in USA in 1929.

Year	History	Culture
1899	Aspirin introduced.	Strauss, *Der Rosenkavalier*.
1911	Chinese revolution against imperial dynasty.	Joyce, *Dubliners*. Ezra Pound, *Des Imagistes*.
1914	First World War begins. Panama Canal opens.	First recording of New Orleans Jazz.
1917	Revolution in Russia. USA declares war on Germany and enters the First World War.	Spengler, *The Decline of the West*.
1918	Armistice Agreement ends the First World War.	Charlie Chaplin, Douglas Fairbanks, D. W. Griffith and Mary Pickford form United Artists.
1919	Treaty of Versailles. In US, Prohibition begins.	Pirandello, *Six Characters in Search of an Author*.
1921	Chinese Communist Party founded.	T. S. Eliot, *The Waste Land*. Joyce, *Ulysses*.
1922	Soviet Union formed. Benito Mussolini's fascists march on Rome.	Le Corbusier, *Vers une architecture*. Sean O'Casey, *The Shadow of a Gunman*.

Year	Age	Life
1923	24	Appeared in the revue *London Calling!* Wrote *The Vortex*, produced in Britain in 1924 and in USA in 1925, and *Fallen Angels*, produced in Britain in 1925 and USA in 1927.
1924	25	Directed and appeared in *The Vortex* in London. Wrote *Hay Fever*, produced in Britain and USA in 1925, and *Easy Virtue*, produced in USA in 1925 and Britain in 1926.
1925	26	Continued appearing in *The Vortex* in London and also in USA. Wrote book, music and lyrics for *On With the Dance*, produced that year in Britain.
1926	27	Wrote *This Was a Man*, produced in that year in USA, *The Marquise*, produced in Britain and USA in 1927, and *Semi-Monde*, produced in Britain in 1977.
1927	28	*Easy Virtue*, *The Vortex* and *The Queen Was in the Parlour* filmed. Wrote *Home Chat*, produced in Britain that year and in USA in 1932.
1928	29	Wrote book, music and lyrics for *This Year of Grace!*, produced in Britain and USA that year – also acted in American production.
1929	30	Completed operetta *Bitter Sweet*, produced in Britain and USA that year. Wrote *Private Lives*, produced in Britain and USA in 1930.

Year	History	Culture
1923	Ottoman empire ends. Palestine, Transjordan and Iraq to Britain, Syria to France.	E. M. Forster, *A Passage to India*. T. Mann, *The Magic Mountain*.
1924	Vladimir Lenin dies.	Fitzgerald, *The Great Gatsby*. Kafka, *The Trial*.
1925	Pact of Locarno. Discovery of ionosphere.	Fritz Lang, *Metropolis*. Puccini, *Turandot*. Kafka, *The Castle*.
1926	Germany joins League of Nations. France establishes Republic of Lebanon.	BBC public radio launched. Heidegger, *Being and Time*.
1927	Joseph Stalin comes to power. Lindbergh flies across Atlantic.	Berlioz, *The Taking of Troy*.
1928	Fleming discovers Penicillin. Kellogg-Briand Pact for Peace.	E. Waugh, *Decline and Fall*.
1929	Wall Street crash. European Federal Union proposed.	Faulkner, *The Sound and the Fury*. Woolf, *A Room of One's Own*.

Year	Age	Life
1930	31	Appeared in *Private Lives* in Britain. Wrote *Post Mortem*, first professional production on British television in 1968, and starred in *Cavalcade*.
1931	32	Appeared in *Private Lives* in USA. *Cavalcade* produced in Britain. *Private Lives* filmed.
1932	33	Wrote book, music and lyrics for *Words and Music*, produced in Britain that year. Also wrote *Design for Living*, produced in USA in 1933 and in Britain in 1939. *The Queen Was in the Parlour* filmed again under the title *Tonight is Ours*. *Cavalcade* filmed.
1933	34	Appeared in USA in *Design for Living*. Wrote *Conversation Piece*, produced in Britain and USA in 1934. *Design for Living* and *Bitter Sweet* both filmed.
1934	35	Appeared in *Conversation Piece* in Britain. Wrote *Pointe Valaine*, produced in USA that year and in Britain in 1944.
1935	36	Wrote *Tonight at 8.30*, produced in Britain that year and in USA in 1936. He appeared in both productions.
1937	38	Wrote *Operette*, produced in Britain in 1938. First volume of autobiography, *Present Indicative*, published in Britain and USA.

Year	History	Culture
1930	Gandhi leads Salt March in India. Pluto discovered.	W. H. Auden, *Poems*. T. S. Eliot, *Ash Wednesday*. Faulkner, *As I Lay Dying*.
1931	Spanish republic formed. Building of Empire State Building completed in NY.	Saint-Exupéry, *Vol de nuit*. *City Lights*, starring Chaplin.
1932	Kingdom of Saudi Arabia independent. Kingdom of Iraq independent. Chadwick discovers neutron.	Huxley, *Brave New World*. Romains, *Les homes de bonne volonté*.
1933	Hitler appointed Chancellor of Germany. Roosevelt president in US.	Malraux, *La condition humaine*. Stein, *The Autobiography of Alice B Toklas*.
1934	Long March in China. Enrico Fermi sets off first controlled nuclear reaction.	Agatha Christie, *Murder on the Orient Express*.
1935	In Germany, Nuremberg Laws enacted. Italy invades Ethiopia.	Gershwin, *Porgy and Bess*.
1937	Japan invades China. Photocopier patented in US.	Sartre, *La Nausée*. Steinbeck, *Of Mice and Men*. Picasso, *Guernica*.

Year	Age	Life
1938	39	Adapted *Words and Music* for its American production, entitled *Set to Music*.
1939	40	Wrote *Present Laughter* and *This Happy Breed*. Rehearsals for both interrupted by the war and not produced in Britain until 1942. *Present Laughter* produced in USA in 1946 and *This Happy Breed* in 1949. *To Step Aside* (short stories) published in Britain and USA.
1940	41	Toured Australia and also wrote *Time Remembered* (*Salute to the Brave*), unproduced to date.
1941	42	Wrote and directed *Blithe Spirit*, produced in Britain and USA that year. Wrote screenplay for *In Which We Serve*.
1942	43	Appeared and co-directed (with David Lean) *In Which We Serve*. Toured Britain in *Blithe Spirit*, *Present Laughter* and *This Happy Breed*. *We Were Dancing* (from *Tonight at 8.30*) filmed.
1943	44	Appeared in London in *Present Laughter* and *This Happy Breed*, and co-produced film version of the latter.

Year	History	Culture
1938	Kristallnacht in Germany.	Greene, *Brighton Rock*.
1939	Germany invades Poland. Franco becomes dictator of Spain. Britain and France declare war on Germany.	Steinbeck, *The Grapes of Wrath*. David O Selznick, *Gone with the Wind* with Vivien Leigh and Clark Gable.
1940	Germany occupies France, Belgium, the Netherlands, Norway and Denmark. Churchill becomes Prime Minister. Ravel, *Boléro*. Weill, *The Threepenny Opera*.	Chaplin, *The Great Dictator*. Greene, *The Power and the Glory*.
1941	Germany invades Soviet Union. Churchill and Roosevelt sign Atlantic Charter.	Tippet, 'A Child of Our Time'.
1942	World's first nuclear reactor constructed at the University of Chicago.	Frank Sinatra's stage debut in New York. *Casablanca*, starring Humphrey Bogart and Ingrid Bergman.
1943	Allies bomb Germany. Teheran Conference.	Sartre, *Being and Nothingness*.

Year	Age	Life
1944	45	Toured extensively in South Africa, Far East and Europe. Co-produced film of *Blithe Spirit*. Wrote screenplay for *Brief Encounter* (based on *Still Life* from *Tonight at 8.30*). *Middle East Diary* published in Britain and USA.
1945	46	Wrote *Sigh No More*, produced in Britain that year, and started writing *Pacific 1860*, produced in Britain in 1946.
1946	47	Started writing *Peace In Our Time*, produced in Britain in 1947.
1947	48	Appeared in *Present Laughter* in Britain. Wrote *Long Island Sound*, unproduced to date.
1948	49	Appeared in French production of *Present Laughter* (*Joyeux Chagrins*). Wrote screenplay for *The Astonished Heart* (from *Tonight at 8.30*).
1949	50	Appeared in *The Astonished Heart*. Wrote *Ace of Clubs*, produced in Britain in 1950, and *Home and Colonial*: as *Island Fling* it was produced in USA in 1951 and revised as *South Sea Bubble* in Britain in 1956.

Year	History	Culture
1944	Allies land in Normandy. Paris liberated. Civil war in Greece.	Olivier, *Henry V.* Eisenstein, *Ivan the Terrible.*
1945	Yalta agreement. Germany surrenders. Attlee becomes PM in Britain. Potsdam conference. Atomic bombs dropped on Hiroshima and Nagasaki.	Orwell, *Animal Farm.* Popper, *The Open Society and its Enemies.* Britten, *Peter Grimes.*
1946	Churchill makes 'Iron Curtain' speech.	Sartre, *Existentialism and Humanism.*
1947	Truman Doctrine. India becomes independent.	Tennessee Williams, *A Streetcar Named Desire.*
1948	Marshall Plan. Welfare state created in Britain. Gandhi assassinated.	Brecht, *The Caucasian Chalk Circle* Greene, *The Heart of the Matter.*
1949	NATO formed Republic of Ireland formed. Mao proclaims China a People's Republic.	Orwell, *1984.* De Beauvoir, *The Second Sex.* Miller, *Death of a Salesman.*

Year	Age	Life
1951	52	Wrote *Relative Values*, produced in Britain that year, and *Quadrille*, produced in Britain in 1952 and in USA in 1954. Made first cabaret appearance at Café de Paris, London. *Star Quality* (short stories) published in Britain and USA.
1952	53	Three plays from *Tonight at 8.30* filmed as *Meet Me Tonight*.
1953	54	Wrote *After The Ball*, produced in Britain in 1954 and in USA in 1955.
1954	55	Wrote *Nude With Violin*, produced in Britain in 1956 and USA in 1957. *Future Indefinite* published in Britain and USA.
1955	56	Cabaret season in Las Vegas, USA. Wrote and appeared in *Together With Music* for US television.
1956	57	Appeared in *Blithe Spirit* and *This Happy Breed* on US television. Wrote *Volcano*, unproduced to date.
1957	58	Appeared in USA in *Nude With Violin*.

Year	History	Culture
1951	Anzus pact in Pacific.	J D Salinger, *The Catcher in the Rye.* Welles, *Othello.*
1952	Elizabeth II becomes Queen.	Beckett, *Waiting for Godot.*
1953	Stalin dies. Double helix (DNA) discovered Welles, *Citizen Kane.* Brecht, *Mother Courage and her Children.*	Miller, *The Crucible.* Thomas, *Under Milk Wood.*
1954	Colour television service begins in US.	Tolkein, *The Lord of the Rings.*
1955	West Germany joins NATO. Warsaw Pact formed.	Vladimir Nabokov, *Lolita.*
1956	Suez Crisis. Fidel Castro and Ché Guevara land in Cuba.	Elvis Presley, *Heartbreak Hotel, Love me tender.*
1957	EEC formed.	Bernstein / Sondheim, *West Side Story.*

Year	Age	Life
1958	59	Appeared in USA in *Present Laughter* and *Nude With Violin*. Adapted Feydau's *Occupe-tois d'Amelie* as *Look After Lulu*, produced in USA and Britain in 1959. Composed score for the ballet *London Morning*, produced in Britain in 1959.
1959	60	Wrote *Waiting in the Wings*, produced in Britain in 1960.
1960	61	Novel *Pomp and Circumstance* published in Britain and USA.
1961	62	Completed *Sail Away*, produced in the USA that year and in Britain in 1962.
1962	63	Wrote music and lyrics for *The Girl Who Came to Supper*, produced in USA in 1963.
1964	65	Directed *High Spirits* (musical of *Blithe Spirit*) in USA and *Hay Fever* in Britain. *Pretty Polly Barlow* (short stories) published in Britain.
1965	66	Wrote *Suite in Three Keys*, produced in Britain in 1960 and (as *Noel Coward in Two Keys*) in USA in 1974.
1966	67	Appeared in Britain in *Suite In Three Keys*.

Year	History	Culture
1958	Pope John XXIII elected. Texas Instruments invent silicon chip.	Pasternack, *Dr. Zhivago*. Pinter, *The Birthday Party*.
1959	In US, Alaska and Hawaii are admitted to the Union.	Motown Records founded.
1960	Vietnam War begins.	Hitchcock, *Psycho*.
1961	Berlin Wall erected. Yuri Gagarin is first man in space.	Rolling Stones are formed.
1962	Cuban Missile Crisis. Satellite television launched.	Albee, *Who's afraid of Virginia Woolf?*
1964	Civil Rights Act in US. Word processor invented.	Kubrick, *Doctor Strangelove*.
1965	Military coup in Indonesia. Indo-Pakistan War.	Beach Boys, *California Girls*. Pinter, *The Homecoming*.
1966	Gandhi becomes PM of India.	Graham Greene, *The Comedians*.

Year	Age	Life
1967	68	Wrote *Bon Voyage* (short stories) and *Not Yet the Dodo* (verses) published in Britain and USA.
1970	71	Received knighthood in the British New Years Honours List.
1972	73	*Cowardy Custard* produced in Britain and *Oh, Coward!* in USA.
1973	74	Died on 26 March in Jamaica.

Year	History	Culture
1967	Six Day War. First heart transplant.	Beatles, *Sargeant Pepper's Lonely Hearts Club Band.*
1970	Northern Ireland riots.	Jimi Hendrix dead.
1972	Bloody Sunday massacre. World Trade Center completed.	Coppola, *The Godfather.*
1973	Denmark, Ireland and Britain enter EEC.	Pink Floyd, *The Dark Side of the Moon.*

Further Reading

Braybrooke, Patrick, *The Amazing Mr Coward*, Archer, London, 1933.

Briers, Richard, *Coward and Company*, Robson, London, 1987.

Greacen, Robert, *The Art of Noel Coward*, Hand & Flower Press, England, 1953.

Mander, Raymond and Mitchenson, Joe, *Theatrical Companion to Coward*, Rockliff, London, 1957.

Payn, Graham, *My Life with Noel Coward*, Applause, New York, 1994.

Richard, Dick (ed), *The Wit of Noel Coward*, Leslie Frewin, London, 1968.

List of Works

Withered Nosegay (satire), Christopher's, London, 1922.

Terribly Intimate Portraits (satire), Boni and Liverright, New York, 1922.

Three Plays (with the author's reply to his critics), Ernest Benn, London, 1925.

Chelsea Buns (satire), Hutchinson, London, 1925.

Three Plays with a Preface, Martin Secker, London, 1925.

The Plays of Noel Coward (Preface by Arnold Bennett), Doubleday, Doran, New York, 1928.

Bitter-Sweet and Other Plays (Preface by Somerset Maugham), Doubleday, Doran, New York, 1929.

Collected Sketches and Lyrics, Hutchinson, London, 1931.

Spangled Unicorn (satire), Hutchinson, London, 1932.

Play Parade Volumes 1–6, Heinemann, London, 1934–1962.

Present Indicative (autobiography), Heinemann, London, 1937.

To Step Aside (short stories), Heinemann, London, 1939.

Australia Visited 1940 (broadcasts), Heinemann, London, 1941.

Middle East Diary (autobiography), Heinemann, London, 1944.

Star Quality (short stories), Heinemann, London, 1951.

The Noel Coward Song Book, Michael Joseph, London, 1953.

Future Indefinite (autobiography), Heinemann, London, 1954.

Pomp and Circumstance (novel), Heinemann, London, 1960.

The Collected Short Stories, Heinemann, London, 1962.

Pretty Polly Barlow (short stories), Heinemann, London, 1964.

3 Plays by Noel Coward (preface by Edward Albee), Delta, Dell
  Publishing Co Inc, New York 1965.
The Lyrics of Noel Coward, Heinemann, London, 1965.
Suite in Three Keys (plays), Heinemann, London, 1966.
Bon Voyage (short stories), Heinemann, London, 1967.
Not Yet The Dodo (verse), Heinemann, London, 1967.

Picture Sources

The author and publishers wish to express their thanks to the following sources of illustrative material and/or permission to reproduce it. They will make proper acknowledgements in future editions in the event that any omissions have occurred.

Album akg Images: pp. 85, 116, 141; Getty Images: pp. 5, 32, 40, 49, 81, 85, 97, 99, 101, 108, 115, 119, 121, 139, 143, 145; Lebrecht Picture Library: pp. 23, 51, 59, 69, 76, 155; Marlene Dietrich Collection, Film Museum Berlin: p. 112. Mary Evans Picture Library: pp. i, iii, v; Topham Picturepoint: pp. 9, 15, 21, 25, 27, 30, 37, 63, 94, 110, 123, 125, 130.

Acknowledgements

My thanks are due first to Paul Webb for his sustained help in keeping this book within the format desired; I would also like to thank my darling and patient wife, Ruth Leon (another author in this series), and of course our equally patient publisher Barbara Schwepcke. Thanks are also due to the Noel Coward Estate and to Methuen for allowing me to quote extracts from the Noel Coward verse, lyrics, autobiographies and plays, all of which they publish.

Index

Adelphi, the, 54, 72
Agate, James, 35
Aitken, Maria, 148–50
America, 29, 37, 46, 69, 72, 74–6,
    100, 103, 114, 116–7, 121, 130,
    142
Andrews, Robert, 8
Annis, Francesca, 150
Apple Cart, The, 110
April, Elsie, 15
Arc De Triomphe, 106
Arlen, Michael, 19
Art, 118
Artists' Rifles, 13–4
Astaire, Fred, 15, 28, 64
Auden, W H, 72

Bacall, Lauren, 125
Bankhead, Tallulah, 24, 33
Bannerman, Margaret, 33
Barrie, J M, 66
Battersea, 3, 7, 138
Beaton, Cecil, 109, 140
Beerbohm, Max, 136
Berlin, 36, 38
Berlin, Irving, 16
Best, Edna, 23, 33, 37
Billy Rose Theatre, New York, 141
Birmingham Rep, 19
Birth of a Nation, The, 11
Blezard, William, 148
Blitz, the, 77–8

Bogarde, Sir Dirk, 137
Bond, Gary, 148
Boucicault, Nina, 39
Bourne, Bette, 150
Braithwaite, Lilian, 32
Brief Encounter, 9, 65, 93, 126,
    129, 151
Broadway, 24, 26, 38, 46, 50, 58, 69,
    97, 100, 117, 125–6, 130, 133,
    140, 149
Browning Version, The, 111
Buchanan, Jack, 28
Burton, Richard, 50, 140, 149

Cadell, Simon, 148–9
Café de Paris, 104, 109, 112
Caine, Michael, 124
Calthrop, Gladys, 23, 51, 85, 97,
    105, 143
Cambridge Theatre, the, 103
Campbell, Judy, 77, 82
Cantinflas, 116
Careless Rapture, 106
Carey, Joyce, 81, 85, 143, 145
Chamberlain, Neville, 73, 75
Charlot, Andre, 26–7
Chester, Betty, 19
Churchill, Winston, 74–5, 95, 102,
    139
Cochran's 1931 Revue, 50, 54
Cohen, Jonathan, 149
Colman, Ronald, 24

Colonial Theatre, Boston, 126
Comden, Betty, 61
Comedy, the, 149
Connery, Sean, 125
Connolly, Cyril, 68, 96
Conti, Tom, 83
Cooper, Duff, 75
Cooper, Gladys, 29, 33, 104
Courtneidge, Cicely, 105, 133
Courtneidge, Robert, 26
Coward, Eric, 4, 7
Coward, Noel: birth, 1, 4; mother, 6,
    14, 67, 76, 114; father, 3, 4, 10,
    19, 67; boy actor, 3–6; death of
    brother, 4; early childhood, 4–7,
    67; audition for *The Goldfish*, 6;
    teenage years, 7–10; early drive for
    attention, 11; call up, 12–3; first
    film, 11; incipient TB, 13; early
    works 15–20; limited ability to
    read music, 16; workaholic, 18–9;
    returns to theatre, 19; the Roaring
    Twenties, 21–46; first trip abroad,
    22; first trip to New York, 23–6;
    American visits and productions,
    23–6, 28–9, 35–8, 41, 46, 50,
    56–8, 61,69, 74–6, 88, 100, 114,
    116–7, 121–2, 130, 141–3; revue
    debut in West End, 26; prolific
    early output, 26–9; first hit song,
    28; country house circuit, 30;
    biggest break, 30; Lord
    Chamberlain, 31, 36; media storm,
    33–4; first premiere in New York,
    35; three plays open in West End,
    38; two disasters, 39–41; plays into
    films, 41; royal seal of approval, 42;
    the stylish 1930s, 47–72; *Private
    Lives* acclaimed, 47–50; patriotic
    works, 51–3, 78–80; sexuality, 22,
    24, 26, 36, 44–5, 58, 60, 84, 127,
    135–7; second film appearance, 61;
    royal connections, 61–3, 122–3,
    125, 143; nine one-act plays, 63–7;
    first autobiography, 67–8; friendly
    rivalry with Ivor Novello, 71–2,
    97–101, 105–7; propaganda effort,
    72–7; wartime productions, 77–96;
    cinema career takes off, 85–6;
    entertaining the troops, 88; surviv-
    ing the peace, 97–102; solo per-
    former, 104, 109, 112–6; tribute to
    Gertrude Lawrence, 107; second
    autobiography, 114; concert on tel-
    evision, 117; tax exile, 87, 118;
    late flowering of talents, 124–31;
    later films, 116–7, 121, 124, 133,
    140–1; life in Jamaica, 127,
    137–40, 145; televised plays, 131;
    final public appearances, 144;
    awarded knighthood, 152; death,
    145–7
PLAYS – AUTHOR: *The Astonished
    Heart*, 65, 67, 101; *Barriers Down*,
    22; *Blithe Spirit*, 10, 81, 82, 93,
    117, 131, 133, 149; *Cavalcade*, 1,
    21, 51–3, 58, 72, 78, 83, 86, 106,
    150; *Come Into the Garden, Maud*,
    133; *Design for Living*, 9, 24,
    58–60, 131–2; *Downhill*, 40; *Easy
    Virtue*, 29, 33, 35–6, 41; *Fallen
    Angels*, 29, 33–4, 38, 59, 117;
    Fumed Oak, 66; *Hay Fever*, 24, 29,
    33–5, 50, 58–9, 83, 132–3, 143,
    150; *High Spirits*, 130, 133; *Home
    Chat*, 38, 39; *I'll Leave It to You*, 20,
    22, 26; *The Impossible Wife*, 35; *The
    Last Trick*, 18–19, 35; *Look After
    Lulu*, 121–2; *The Marquise*, 38, 39;
    Nude With Violin, 117–8, 121, 137;
    Occupy Yourself With Amelia, 122; *On
    With the Dance*, 33; *Point Valaine*,
    61, 100; *Present Laughter*, 10, 59,
    82–4, 88, 100, 119, 131, 137;

Private Lives, 1, 9–10, 21, 32, 34, 46–7, 50–1, 58–9, 63, 66, 82, 100, 106–7, 132, 135, 141, 149; *Quadrille*, 107, 109, 114; *The Queen Was in the Parlour*, 35–6, 58; *The Rat Trap*, 18, 35; *Red Peppers*, 64–6; *Relative Values*, 104–5; *Semi-Monde*, 150; *Shadow Play*, 64, 66–7; *Shadows of the Evening*, 133; *Sigh No More*, 91; *Sirocco*, 24, 38, 39, 40; *Song at Twilight*, 124, 133, 135–6; *South Sea Bubble*, 117, 138; *Still Life*, 9, 66, 93; *Suite in Three Keys*, 133, 136–7; *This Happy Breed*, 82–3, 88, 117; *This Was a Man*, 36, 38; *Tonight at 8.30*, 63–7, 86, 93, 100, 109; *The Vortex*, 1, 23, 29–33, 35, 37, 41, 68, 83, 120, 131, 150; *Waiting in the Wings*, 124; *We Were Dancing*, 66, 86; *A Withered Nosegay*, 23; *The Young Idea*, 23–4, 26

PLAYS – ACTOR or DIRECTOR: *Androcles and the Lion*, 140; *The Constant Nymph*, 37; *George and Margaret*, 69; *The Goldfish*, 6, 8; *The Great Name*, 7; *The Knight of the Burning Pestle*, 19, 23; *Peter Pan*, 6; *Polly With a Past*, 23; *The Royal Family*, 61; *The Saving Grace*, 12; *Scandal*, 16–17; *War in the Air*, 8; *Where the Rainbow Ends*, 8; *Wild Heather*, 12

SONGS: Alice Is At It Again, 99–100; Any Little Fish, 50; A Bar on the Piccolo Marina, 129, 145; Could You Please Oblige Us With a Bren Gun?, 79; Don't Let's Be Beastly to the Germans, 80; Forbidden Fruit, 15; Green Carnation, 45; Half-Caste Woman, 50; Has Anybody Seen Our Ship?, 64; Home Sweet Heaven, 133; I Like America, 103; I Wonder What Happened to Him, 92; If Love Were All, 43–4, 151; I'll Follow My Secret Heart, 60; I'll See You Again, 10, 43–4; London Pride, 3, 42, 78, 118, 151; Mad About the Boy, 56–7, 135; Mad Dogs and Englishmen, 54–5, 70, 74, 152; Matelot, 92–3; Men About Town, 64; Mrs Worthington, 42; Parisian Pierrot, 27; The Party's Over Now, 55; A Room With a View, 41, 42; Sail Away, 103; Saturday Night at the Rose and Crown, 131; Someday I'll Find You, 10, 48; The Stately Homes of England, 3, 42, 69–71, 118; Tamarisk Town, 15; There Are Bad Times Just Around the Corner, 95–6; Twentieth Century Blues, 52–3, 106; Uncle Harry, 98; Where Are the Songs We Sung?, 69–70; Why Must the Show Go On?, 144; World Weary, 42, 43; You Were There, 64–5

REVUES & MUSICALS: *Ace of Clubs*, 103; *After the Ball*, 110–2, 124; *Bitter Sweet*, 1, 43, 45, 58, 69, 72; *Conversation Piece*, 60, 69; *Cowardy Custard*, 141, 143, 148; *Crissa*, 22; *The Girl Who Came to Supper*, 130–1; *The Globe Review*, 109; *London Calling!*, 26–7; *The Lyric Revue*, 104; *Noel Coward's Sweet Potato*, 141; *Oh Coward!*, 141, 143, 148; *Operette*, 69–72; *Pacific 1860*, 97–9, 138; *Sail Away*, 124, 126, 128, 130; *This Year of Grace*, 41, 42; *Together With Music*, 117; *Words and Music*, 54, 56

FILMS: *Around the World in 80*

Days, 116–7; *Boom*, 140–1; *Bunny Lake is Missing*, 124, 133, 141; *Hearts of the World*, 1, 11; *In Which We Serve*, 1, 85–8; *The Italian Job*, 124, 141; *Meet Me Tonight*, 109; *Our Man in Havana*, 121; *The Scoundrel*, 12, 61; *We Were Dancing*, 86
POEMS: *The Boy Actor*, 3; *Happy New Year*, 88–9; *I Am No Good at Love*, 152; *Lie in the Dark and Listen*, 89–90, 151
BOOKS: *Bon Voyage*, 140; *Cherry Pan*, 17; *Future Indefinite*, 114; *Middle East Diary*, 88; *Pomp and Circumstance*, 17, 125; *Present Indicative*, 67–8
SCREENPLAY: *Concerto*, 41
Crest of the Wave, 106
Criterion, the, 38
Crystal Palace, the, 6

Daily Express, 37
Daily Mail, 66
Dancing Years, The, 106, 111
Dare, Zena, 101
Darewski, Herman, 17–18
Darewski, Max, 17–18
Dasto, Dany, 151
Dean, Basil, 36–7, 40
Delysia, 17
Denville Hall, 124–5
Desert Inn, Las Vegas, 116
Devine, Laurie, 41
Dexter, John, 132,
Dietrich, Marlene, 104–5, 112, 140, 144, 148
Doble, Frances, 40
Donmar, the, 148, 150
Douglas, Melvyn, 86
Drury Lane, 21, 72, 106
Du Maurier, Sir Gerald, 120

Dullea, Keir, 133
Duncan, Lindsay, 149

Eagles, Jeanne, 23
Ebury Street, 12–13, 18
Edgar, David, 151
Ejiofor, Chiwetel, 150
Ellis, Mary, 106, 111
Entertainer, The, 119
Enthoven, Gabrielle, 24
Erlanger's, 46
Evans, Dame Edith, 23, 132
Evening Standard, The, 34, 109, 119, 149
Everyman Theatre, Hampstead, 18, 30, 35

Fellowes, Julian, 107
Fenn, Jean, 126
Ferrer, Jose, 130
Feydeau, 121–2
Fiander, Lewis, 148
Field, Lila, 6, 8
Finney, Albert, 83
First World War, 6–7, 11, 17, 62, 80
Fleming, Ian, 138
Fleming, Lucy, 151
Folliot, Gladys, 17
Fontanne, Lynn, 24, 58–60, 107, 109
Fox, Edward, 151
French, Harold, 8, 19
Fresnay, Pierre, 60
Front Page, The, 61

Gabor, Zsa Zsa, 115
Gaiety, the, Manchester, 20
Garrick, the, 150
Gay's the Word, 105, 107
Gershwin Theatre, Broadway, 150
Gibbons, Caroll, 77
Gielgud, John, 35, 37–8, 63, 116–9, 135

Gilbert and Sullivan, 10
Gish, Dorothy, 1, 11–12
Gish, Lilian, 1, 11–12
Glamorous Night, 106
Glasgow Citizens Theatre, 150
Globe, the, 117
Goldenhurst in Kent, 51, 139
Goldfish, The, 6, 8
Gosford Park, 107
Granada Television, 131
Grandage, Michael, 150
Gray, Timothy, 130, 133
Green, Adolph, 61
Greene, Graham, 81, 121
Gregg, Hubert, 151
Grenfell, Joyce, 108
Griffith, D W, 1, 11–12
Grimes, Tammy, 122, 131, 133
Groener, Harry, 149
Guildhall School of Music, 15

Hackforth, Norman, 104
Hale, Sonnie, 41
Halifax, Lord, 73
Hall, Sir Peter, 59
Hammond, Kay, 81
Harris, Rosemary, 125
Harrison, Rex, 81, 117
Hart, Moss, 67, 76
Hawtrey, Charles, 7–8, 19
Hayward, Louis, 135
Hecht, Ben, 12, 61
Helen Hayes Theatre, New York, 143
Helpmann, Robert, 76, 119
Hemingway, Ernest, 121
Henderson, Florence, 130
Henry Miller Theatre, 33
Henry V, 106
Her Majesty's, 43
Hirst, Joan, 85
His Majesty's, 69

Hitchcock, Alfred, 12, 41
Hodge, Patricia, 148–9
Holmesdale, Jeffrey (Lord Amherst), 24, 54
Hope, Anthony, 36
Howard, Trevor, 9, 93–4, 126
Hunt, Martita, 133

If Love Were All, 149
Illustrated London News, The, 23, 51
Intolerance, 11
Isherwood, Christopher, 72

Jacobi, Derek, 132
Jamaica, 84, 125, 127, 137–8, 140, 142, 145–6, 150, 153
Jayston, Michael, 149
John Murray Anderson's Almanac, 46
Johnson, Celia, 9, 67, 93–4, 129, 151

Kaufman and Hart, 61
Keith, Penelope, 82, 149
Kendal, Kay, 108
Kennedy, Jackie, 126
Kennedy, Margaret, 37
Kern, Jerome, 16, 117
Kings Head Theatre, Islington, 136, 148
Kingsway Theatre, 23
Kipling, Rudyard, 152

Lang, Robert, 133
Lathom, Ned, 26
Lawrence, Gertrude, 1, 3, 4, 6, 9–10, 19, 27–8, 48, 63, 65, 67, 76, 100–1, 107, 109, 117, 148
Lawson, Leigh, 149
Laye, Evelyn, 46
Lee, Vanessa, 101, 111
Leigh, Vivien, 75, 117, 122
Leighton, Margaret, 67, 108

Lesley, Cole, 84, 139–40, 145–6
Lillie, Bea, 133
Lodger, The, 12
London Calling!, 26–7
London Coliseum, 107
Look Back in Anger, 119–20
Lord Chamberlain, 31
Lorn, Loraine, 84
Losey, Jo, 141
Lumley, Joanna, 148
Lunt, Alfred, 24, 58–60, 107, 109
Lyric, the, 117

MacArthur, Charles, 12, 61
Macdermott, Norman, 30
MacLiammoir, Michael, 6
Manners, Hartley, 24, 29
Markham, Kika, 136
Marryot, Jane, 52
Martin, Hugh, 130, 133
Martin, Mary, 98–9, 117
Massey, Anna, 133
Maugham, Somerset, 127, 136
Meet Me Tonight, 109
Melville, Alan, 105
Menzies, Bob, 77
Merry Widow, The, 106
Messel, Oliver, 140
Miguel (Coward's housekeeper), 146
Miller, Arthur, 151
Miller, Gilbert, 18–20
Moffat, John, 148
Monroe, Marilyn, 130
Morosco, the, 69
Mountbatten, Lord Louis, 86, 127, 142–3
Mrs Dale's Diary, 41
My Life With Noel Coward, 145

National Film Theatre, 142
National Theatre, the, 12, 124, 132, 149

Neagle, Anna, 119
Nesbit, E S, 146
New Statesman, 68
New Theatre (the Albery), 22, 122, 150
New York, 23–6, 28–9, 33, 35–6, 38, 41, 46, 50, 56, 61, 67, 72, 74–6, 88, 97, 114, 119, 121–2, 142–3, 150–1
Nichols, Beverly, 68
Noel and Gertie, 148–9
Noel Coward Estate, 1
Noel Coward Society, 61, 151
Noel Coward Study Centre, 151
Novello, Ivor, 23, 39, 40, 41, 63, 68, 72, 85, 88, 97–8, 101, 105–6, 138

Oberon, Merle, 144
Observer, The, 39, 42
Olivier, Lawrence, 75, 87, 124, 130, 132–3, 142
Olympia Theatre, Dublin, 117
Osborne, John, 119–20
O'Shea, Tessie, 130–1
O'Toole, Peter, 83

Palermo, 36
Palmer, Lilli, 136
Paris, 22, 36, 73, 74
Patrick, Nigel, 83
Pavilion, the, 33
Payn, Graham, 84, 93, 100–1, 135, 140, 145–6, 151
Peter Pan, 6
Phoenix, the, 50, 63, 106–7, 109, 142
Piccadilly Theatre, 91
Pinter, Harold, 47
Playfair, Nigel, 19, 23
Playhouse Theatre, Liverpool, 107
Poppy Pierrots, The, 10

Porter, Cole, 68
Powell, Jane, 115
Prince and the Showgirl, The, 130
Prince of Wales theatre, the, 7
Printemps, Yvonne, 60
Prisoner of Zenda, The, 36
Prowse, Philip, 150

Queen Elizabeth the Queen Mother, 62, 122–3, 125, 143, 151

Rains, Claude, 23
Rattigan, Terence, 42, 112, 120, 130, 132
Reagan, Nancy, 41
Redgrave, Corin, 136
Redgrave, Lynn, 132
Redgrave, Michael, 101
Redgrave, Vanessa, 136
Reed, Carol, 121–2
Relph, Michael, 105
Reza, Yasmina, 118
Rickman, Alan, 149
Robertson, Liz, 148
Rodgers, Richard, 140
Rodgers and Hammerstein, 117
Rogers, Ginger, 64
Roosevelt, Franklin D, 74
Routledge, Patricia, 148
Royal Court, the, 120, 122
Royalty, the, 33
Rutherford, Margaret, 93, 117, 149

Savory, Gerald, 69
Savoy theatre, the, 82, 104, 149
Second World War, 10, 13, 21, 54, 138
Shakespeare, William, 151
Shaw, George Bernard, 66, 110
Shearer, Norma, 86
Shulman, Milton, 149
Sitwells (Edith, Osbert and Sachaverell), 23, 29
Sleeping Prince, The, 130
Smith, C Aubrey, 23
Smith, Maggie, 132–3, 141, 149
Spectator, The, 81
St James's Theatre, 23
St Martin's, the, 35
Standing, John, 141, 149
Stephens, Robert, 141, 149
Stern, G B, 16
Stopes, Marie, 26
Strachan, Alan, 149
Stritch, Elaine, 126, 130
Stuart, Sir Campbell, 73, 75
Sunday Times, The, 35
'Swiss Family Whittlebot, The', 29
Switzerland, 137, 142

Talent To Amuse, A, 2, 44, 142
Tappe, Horst, 155
Taylor, Elizabeth, 50, 140, 149
Taylor, Laurette, 24, 29
Teddington, 11, 67, 138
Tempest, Marie, 29, 38, 39
Theatre Museum, 24
Theatre Royal, Bath, 59
Theatre Royal, Drury Lane, 51, 61, 97, 150
Theatre Royal, Haymarket, 88, 100
Times Literary Supplement, The, 50
Times, The, 65, 82, 117
Titheradge, Madge, 29, 33
Todd, Michael, 116
Tonge, Philip, 8
Twiggy, 149
Tynan, Kenneth, 6, 109, 120, 132
Tyson, Lynden, 14

Waters of the Moon, 105
Waugh, Evelyn, 96
Webb, Alan, 84, 135
Webb, Paul, 2

West End, 26, 38, 46, 58, 61–3, 66, 82, 126, 130, 135–6, 140, 149
West, Rebecca, 101
Wilde, Oscar, 50, 111, 151
Wilding, Michael, 119
Williams, Emelyn, 67
Williams, Simon, 151
Williams, Tennessee, 140
Willmore, Alfred, 6
Wilson, Harold, 142
Wilson, Jack, 36, 84, 133

Windsor, Duke and Duchess of, 122–3
Winn, Godfrey, 68
Winter, Mark, 148
Wood, Peggy, 46
Woods, Al, 19
Woodward, Edward, 133
Worth, Irene, 136
Wynne, Esme, 10–11, 14, 17

Ziegfeld Theatre, Broadway, 46

Alexander the Great
by Nigel Cawthorne
'moves through the career at a brisk,
dependable canter in his pocket
biography for Haus.'
BOYD TONKIN, *The Independent*
ISBN 1-904341-56-X (pb) £9.99

Armstrong
by David Bradbury
'it is a fine and well-researched
introduction'
GEORGE MELLY *Daily Mail*
ISBN 1-904341-46-2 (pb) £8.99

Bach
by Martin Geck
'The production values of the book
are exquisite.' *Guardian*
ISBN 1-904341-16-0 (pb) £8.99
ISBN 1-904341-35-7 (hb) £12.99

Beethoven
by Martin Geck
'...this little gem is a truly handy
reference.' *Musical Opinion*
ISBN 1-904341-00-4 (pb) £8.99
ISBN 1-904341-03-9 (hb) £12.99

Bette Davis
by Laura Moser
'The author compellingly unearths
the complex, self-destructive woman
that lay beneath the steely persona
of one of the best-loved actresses of
all time.'
ISBN 1-904341-48-9 (pb) £9.99

Bevan
by Clare Beckett
and Francis Beckett
"Haus, the enterprising new
imprint, adds another name to its
list of short biographies ... a timely
contribution.'
GREG NEALE, *BBC History*
ISBN 1-904341-63-2 (pb) £9.99

Brahms
by Hans A Neunzig
'These handy volumes fill a gap in
the market for readable,
comprehensive and attractively
priced biographies admirably.'
JULIAN HAYLOCK, *Classic fm*
ISBN 1-904341-17-9 (pb) £8.99